Your
Horoscope
2020

....

Pisces

Your Horoscope 2020

....

Pisces

20th February - 20th March

igloobooks

igloobooks

Published in 2019
by Igloo Books Ltd
Cottage Farm
Sywell
NN6 0BJ
www.igloobooks.com

0819 001.01
2 4 6 8 10 9 7 5 3 1
ISBN 978-1-78905-716-4

Written by Belinda Campbell and Denise Evans

Cover design by Dave Chapman
Edited by Bobby Newlyn-Jones

Printed and manufactured in China

CONTENTS

INTRODUCTION
....

This horoscope has been specifically created to allow
you to get the most from astrological patterns and
the way they have a bearing on not only your zodiac
sign, but nuances within it. Using the diary section
of the book you can read about the influences and
possibilities of each and every day of the year. It will
be possible for you to see when you are likely to be
cheerful and happy or those times when your nature
is in retreat and you will be more circumspect. The
diary will help to give you a feel for the specific
'cycles' of astrology and the way they can subtly
change your day-to-day life.

THE CHARACTER OF
THE TWO FISH
. . . .

Compassionate, creative, and charitable, Pisceans are
the visionary dreamers who can breathe magic into the
world. Whether it's their love of illusions like Derren
Brown or their wonderful world building talents like
Dr. Seuss, the enchanting Pisces can help bring joy and
expand the minds of others. Neptune and Jupiter co-rule
Pisces and provide this sign with a limitless imagination
and a thirst for growth. At times, Pisceans can get lost
in their fantasies and become detached from reality.
A helping hand of support and encouragement from
their friends and family might be needed to bring a lost
Pisces back to reality. Wherever a Piscean's passion lies,
however, their imagination will shine through, from Paul
Hollywood's baking, to Michelangelo's Sistine Chapel
and even to Albert Einstein's Theory of Relativity.
A Piscean's negative energy means that they can
be more focused on their internal growth than on
experiencing external stimulus. This means that mental,
spiritual, and emotional journeys are where this sign
most likes to travel. The Two Fish that symbolise this
sign can hint at a dual and slippery nature that makes
this elusive siren of the sea hard to pin down. As a
Water sign that is governed by their emotions, they can
get carried away on a fast-moving current and should
be careful not to drown their loved ones in their, at
times, overwhelming excitement. Belonging to the
twelfth house in the zodiac calendar where sacrifice and

devotion are key, there is surely no sign that is more generous with their time and love than pious Pisces. However, this sign should be careful that their self-sacrificing tendencies don't turn them into a martyr, as Pisceans can have a reputation for becoming or playing the victim at times. As the snow begins to melt and the daffodils bloom, mutable Pisceans are born and bring with them a wise understanding of what has come before. Born at the end of winter and the end of the zodiac calendar, Pisces can be the most adaptable and understanding of all the signs, having learnt something from each of the star signs before them.

THE TWO FISH

Symbolised by the Two Fish, Pisces is one of the signs of the zodiac calendar with a dual symbol. The duality of Pisces could suggest flexibility in their emotions; getting excited for a project one day and bored the next may be all too familiar to many Pisceans. But being the last of the Water signs, the Two Fish of Pisces can be capable of exploring the true depth and stretch of their emotions, encompassing both the allure of seductive Scorpio and sensitivity from family orientated Cancer. These slippery Fish can try and wriggle their way out of tight spots, coming up with the most fantastical of fibs. But if a reluctant Piscean constantly swims away from the truth, they may end up going in circles like their symbol of the Two Fish chasing each other's tales. This sign should try to remember that by accepting their slip-ups they can then learn from them and avoid making the same mistakes in the future.

JUPITER AND NEPTUNE

Co-ruled by the largest planet in the sky, Jupiter, and imaginative Neptune, Pisceans can certainly dream big. Jupiter, the ruler of the Gods in Roman mythology, ruled over the sky whilst his brother Neptune ruled the seas. This suggests that Pisceans can be a double force to be reckoned with. At times dreamy, Pisceans may have their heads stuck in their Jupiter clouds and at others they can feel as deeply as Neptune's waters and be as elusive and mythical as a mermaid. Jupiter is the fastest spinning planet in the solar system resulting in it having the shortest days of all the planets, which a tardy Piscean might be quick to blame for their lateness. Pisceans can be incredibly understanding, but when pushed too far their anger can be as tempestuous as the sea of their co-ruler Neptune. Neptune is associated with spiritual intuition and its rule can help guide this compassionate Water sign to better understand the world, whilst adventurous Jupiter can help them explore and find their place within it.

ELEMENTS, MODES AND POLARITIES

Each sign is made up of a unique combination of three defining groups: elements, modes and polarities. Each of these defining parts can manifest themselves in good and bad ways and none should be seen to be a positive or a negative – including the polarities! Just like a jigsaw puzzle, piecing these groups together can help illuminate why each sign has certain characteristics and help us find a balance.

ELEMENTS

FIRE: Dynamic and adventurous, signs with Fire in them can be extroverted. Others are naturally drawn to them because of the positive light they give off, as well as their high levels of energy and confidence.

Earth: Signs with the Earth element are steady and driven with their ambitions. They make for a solid friend, parent or partner due to their grounded influence and nurturing nature.

Air: The invisible element that influences each of the other elements significantly, Air signs will provide much-needed perspective to others with their fair thinking, verbal skills and key ideas.

Water: Warm in the shallows and freezing as ice. This mysterious element is essential to the growth of everything around it, through its emotional depth and empathy.

MODES

Cardinal: Pioneers of the calendar, cardinal signs jump-start each season and are the energetic go-getters.

Fixed: Marking the middle of the calendar, fixed signs firmly denote and value steadiness and reliability.

Mutable: As the seasons end, the mutable signs adapt and give themselves over gladly to the promise of change.

POLARITIES

Positive: Typically extroverted, positive signs take physical action and embrace outside stimulus in their life.

Negative: Usually introverted, negative signs value emotional development and experiencing life from the inside out.

PISCES IN BRIEF

The table below shows the key attributes of Pisceans.
Use it for quick reference and to understand more about
this fascinating sign.

SYMBOL	RULING PLANET	MODE	ELEMENT	HOUSE
♓	♃ ♆	⌢	▽	XII
Two Fish	Jupiter and Neptune	Mutable	Water	Twelfth

COLOUR	BODY PART	POLARITY	GENDER	POLAR SIGN
		⊖	♀	♍
Sea Green	Feet	Negative	Feminine	Virgo

LOVE

Pisceans are the romantics of the zodiac and will no doubt fantasise about being swept off their feet, just like the starry-eyed characters from their favourite romance novels and films. Their intoxicating imagination and endless generosity rarely fail to charm so they are not likely to be short of admirers. As a mutable and self-sacrificing sign, overly generous Pisceans can be at risk of being too agreeable. Pisces should try not to just be the passenger in their relationships and instead take an active role in their love life. Sitting in the driving seat and taking on more responsibilities, whether it's choosing a restaurant for dinner or sorting out the home insurance, could boost an unsure Piscean's self-confidence and give their partner a needed break from always making the decisions.

As a mutable Water sign, Pisceans can be adaptable to their partner's emotional needs and highly intuitive lovers. A Piscean's mutable quality means that they are also prone to the desire for change, which can have this sign flipping between their emotions and struggling to bind to just the one lover. Symbolised by not one but Two Fish makes Pisces a dual sign that is prone to going back and forth, changing their mind and their feelings. Whilst the Two Fish are deciding on a partner who is best suited to them, they may have a few contenders in the running and they can unintentionally hurt their potential spouses if there is any deceit going on. If this sign can stick to the truth, then they should stand a better chance of staying out of hot water with their lovers. Under the philosophical influence of Jupiter and the spiritualism of Neptune, an easy-going Piscean might have a *que será, será* attitude when it comes to being with someone or not and could be happy to leave it up to the universe to decide for them.

ARIES: COMPATIBILITY 2/5

Dreamy Pisces and action-loving Aries can learn a lot from each other. Watery Pisces can fear delving into the deep end of their desires and prefer to stay in the warmer, shallower waters of their comfort zone, generally choosing to emotionally support their partners' dreams over their own. Aries will want to help Pisces reach their full potential, but Aries should be wary of offending this Water sign as Pisces is known to overflow with emotions when pushed. Pisces can offer much needed emotional support to Aries and the two can form a thoughtful connection deeper than most.

TAURUS: COMPATIBILITY 3/5

Taurus and Pisces are capable of having a highly sympathetic and understanding love. The practically minded Taurus should encourage the dreamy Pisces to live out their fantasies and work hard for themselves, not just others. In return, a Piscean will shower their Taurus in waves of love and gratitude for helping them realise their dreams. However, a Piscean would be wise not to saturate the relationship emotionally and spoil a Taurus. With Pisces being a Water sign, Taureans can feel the nourishing effects this sign has in their Earth element, and the life that these two can grow together is one well worth living.

GEMINI: COMPATIBILITY 3/5

As fluid as water and free flowing as air, Pisces and Gemini can experience an extremely flexible and forgiving relationship when these two fall for each other. Both mutable signs, this couple can be highly compatible and will not fight for leadership but rather rule side by side. Whilst these two may not always perfectly understand each other, their open-minded attitudes will help resolve their disagreements. Whilst Gemini is led by the mind influence of Mercury, contrastingly, the Piscean's influence of Water means that they can be ruled by their emotions. A meeting of the head and heart will be key.

CANCER: COMPATIBILITY 4 /5

These two feminine and Water signs can be a vision of romance together. A Cancerian can truly identify with the changeable river of emotion that runs within Pisces, alternating speeds, directions and temperatures, because the same river runs within them too. Here are two signs that enjoy nurturing their loved ones and so their love will be built on a mutual support system. Be mindful not to drown in the floods of emotions that both the Crab and Fish are capable of unleashing in their romantic relationships so that love and compassion can flow gently.

LEO: COMPATIBILITY 2/5

When Leo meets Pisces, each can bring out the best and worst in each other. Pisces can be a source of emotional encouragement for Leo, whilst Leo can help the dreamy Pisces take more action in their life. This allows them both to realise their dreams. Born in the twelfth house representing sacrifice, Pisces can be selfless whilst Leo, ruled by the Sun, can be the opposite. When these two sacrificing and self-serving characteristics are felt at their extremes, the relationship can turn toxic. However, mutable Pisces and fixed Leo can live in harmony if they both value each other's best qualities.

VIRGO: COMPATIBILITY 5/5

Opposites on the zodiac calendar, hands-on Virgo and mystical Pisces have a loving match but, like any couple, not without their struggles. The slippery Fish symbol of Pisces can hint at an elusiveness that can be attractive or frustrating to steady Earth sign Virgo. Water and Earth are elements that can create beautiful things together, however, in this couple the emotional Piscean and rational Virgo could be a tricky balancing act. These two are deep souls that can empathise and support one another probably better than any other signs and can happily and devotedly serve one another for endless days.

LIBRA: COMPATIBILITY 1/5

Whilst the enigmatic Pisces and suave Libra might be charmed by each other, theirs is a love that could struggle to reach fruition. Cardinal Libras are more likely to be the initiator in this relationship with mutable Pisceans, however, both signs can be struck with an inability to make decisions and this can leave them treading water; neither sinking nor swimming. Libras will be attracted to the artistic side of the creative Piscean and Pisceans are likely to flourish with the encouragement from their positive Libra Partner. Finding a balance between Libra's extrovert and Piscean's introvert nature could allow their romance to bloom.

SCORPIO: COMPATIBILITY 4/5

Here are two Water signs that will go to the ends of the Earth, or rather the depths of the oceans, for one another. Pisceans dream of finding that fantasy love and the enigmatic Scorpio can be just that for them, whilst the empathetic Pisces can be the kindred spirit that secretive Scorpios can finally be vulnerable with. A Piscean's mutable nature which flows with change can be at odds with the steadfast approach of a fixed Scorpio, but their differences mean that they have plenty to learn from each other. Emotional security and sensitivity are where these two thrive.

SAGITTARIUS: COMPATIBILITY 3/5

The roaming Sagittarius and the escapist Pisces could
end up blissfully running off into the sunset together if
they can learn from each other's differences. Both ruled
by Jupiter, these two may indeed have been lucky to find
one another. Jupiter gives Sagittarians and Pisceans a
zest for life and their shared mutable modes will make
their relationship open to continuous growth and change.
Pisceans can lack the active side that many Fire signs
have whilst Sagittarians can lack compassion which
could clash with this sensitive Water sign. By focusing on
common interests, this deep pair could go far.

CAPRICORN: COMPATIBILITY 3/5

An Earth and Water love is bound to be a complimentary
match, and the relationship between a Capricorn and
Piscean may be about helping each other grow as
individuals and flourish as a couple. Capricorn will
bring a practical mind and an active spirit with their
cardinal nature whilst the mutable Piscean will provide
compassion and teach their Goat to be flexible. Both
sides can retreat into themselves in times of great focus
or reflection, particularly Pisceans if their Goat partner
is being overbearing. However, their matching negative
energies could form a deep emotional connection with
each other and demonstrate true patience and dedication.

AQUARIUS: COMPATIBILITY 2/5

Two very giving signs such as Pisces and Aquarius could happily give themselves to each other in love. Whilst an Air and Water sign may struggle to understand one another, an Aquarian's intellect combined with the Piscean's compassion can form a relationship that speaks to both the heart and head if flexibility and patience is practised by the pair. A fixed and mutable combination can be a complimentary match, so long as Aquarians don't try to bend the will of their accommodating Piscean partner. The bond that these two can share when at its best can be sincere and spiritually liberating.

PISCES: COMPATIBILITY 2/5

Two Pisceans might easily capture each other's hearts and imaginations, but their easy-going mutable nature might make their feelings for one another struggle to gain traction and form a solid relationship. However, once these two, or four, Fish decide to commit, their love can be full of thoughtful gift giving and deep emotional understanding. These two Water signs can be sponge-like with both positive and negative energies, so could bring out the best and worst in each other, depending on what they offer to the relationship, but at their shared core is a kind and patient soul.

FAMILY AND FRIENDS

As a Water sign, Pisceans can be incredibly intuitive to the needs of their family and friends, attuned to picking up on even the slightest of changes in their loved one's emotions. A caring Piscean will not think twice about dropping what they are doing to go to a friend's aid, as is their self-sacrificing way. The kind words of a Piscean can help heal many emotional wounds as they will often know just what to say, much to the relief of their family and friends. This eternally compassionate sign is only too glad to give themselves to others that need their support. Kindred spirits for Pisceans are the friends and family that reciprocate their support and encouragement. Fellow Water sign Cancer could be a strong ally with their emotional sensitivity and cardinal go-getter attitude helping Pisceans make their dreams into a reality.

Whilst this sign is devoted to their family and friends, sticking to commitments can be a challenge for many slippery Pisceans. This sign should be wary of overpromising and consequently underdelivering in their eagerness to please and inability to say no. It may seem backwards to a Piscean that by saying 'no' they could strengthen the bonds that they cherish, however, their friends and family are far less likely to get angry if they say they cannot make a date straightaway rather than flaking at the last minute. Time management is a skill that might not come naturally to this sign, but it is a tool that they should learn how to handle so that they can stay on top of their social calendar.

Whilst writing and checking their appointments in a diary or calendar on their phone might not spark the imagination of a Pisces, it will make sure that they don't miss out on spending quality time with their loved ones.

Pisceans can be incredibly creative individuals, and this can be reflected in their enchanting homes. Their walls may be adorned with dreamy watercolour paintings or visitors might be greeted with aromas of burning incense to welcome them into a spiritual Piscean's home. A home by the sea or lake, where a Piscean can see their element of Water regularly, may be where this sign decides to settle. Wherever a Pisces lives geographically, as a parent this sign can feel truly at home. The imaginative Pisces will want to fill their children's childhood with magic and wonder, making sure that Rudolph takes a bite from his carrot on Christmas Eve or leaving a coin and perhaps a tiny note from the Tooth Fairy. Pisceans, whilst not generally materialistic themselves, can be tempted to spoil their children and will always put their children's needs before their own, but they should be careful of giving or doing too much for them. Whether they are a parent, friend, cousin or sister, a Piscean is ready to bring magic to the lives of others and emotionally support their loved ones.

MONEY AND CAREERS

Being a certain star sign will not dictate the type of career that you have, although the characteristics that fall under each sign could help you identify the areas in which you could potentially thrive. Conversely, to succeed in the workplace, it is just as important to understand what you are good at as it is to know what you are less brilliant at so that you can see the areas in which you will need to perhaps work harder in to achieve your career and financial goals.

Whilst Pisceans can have fantastic dreams about what careers they would like to have, they can lack the drive to make their fantasies a reality. A Piscean can get so blissfully lost in thinking about their dream job that they fail to take the necessary steps to reach their goals especially if they are in the habit of underestimating themselves, but building their self-confidence usually helps them to take action. A compatible career path for Pisceans would be something that sparks their imagination and gets their creative juices flowing. Whether it's the music of Rihanna or the paintings of Renoir, a creative Piscean could look to aspirational figures that inspire them to turn their passion into a paid career. Another professional path that Pisces may prefer to follow is one where they can dedicate their time and energy towards improving the lives of others. Born in the twelfth house that signifies service and sacrifice, Pisces can be some of the kindest and most generous of souls, so a caring career as nurse, aid worker, or foster parent could be best suited to the giving Pisces.

When it comes to a Piscean's finances, money can pass through their fingers as quickly as their element Water. This sign will not hesitate to buy something that catches their fancy which can start to be an issue when they unwittingly spend beyond their means. The creative Piscean may have unsteady income and not have much of a grip on their finances and the all too real world of budgets. If the mere thought of spreadsheets is bringing a Piscean out in hives, they would do well to pay for someone else to help with their expenses, particularly if they are self-employed. Earth signs like Taurus, Virgo, and Capricorn will usually have a flair for material things and their practical approach could help a disorganised Pisces handle their money more frugally, helping them establish boundaries to manage their incomings and outgoings. Whilst trusting Pisceans may be tempted to believe in a magical fix to their financial worries, they should avoid any get-rich-quick type schemes as if it sounds too good to be true, it probably is.

Whilst you can't always choose who you work with, it can be advantageous to learn about colleagues' key characteristics through their star signs to try and work out the best ways of working with them. As a Water sign, Pisceans can be swept up in negative and positive energies from their colleagues so it's important for this sign to surround themselves with the latter and guard themselves against the former.

Pisceans truly thrive on positive encouragement, so their neighbouring sign of Aquarius could be the optimistic and creative influence that helps a Piscean to reach their career dreams.

HEALTH AND WELLBEING

....

Pisceans can be the ultimate escapism artists, living in their own fantasy and choosing to be blind to any painful issues in their real life. But even with lucky Jupiter co-ruling this sign, their problems won't often magically fix themselves. If a Piscean feels themselves drifting into escapism, binging on Netflix or playing video games at all hours, then they will need to make a strong conscious effort to come back to reality. Whilst this sign may blame others for their upset state, they could also be a victim of their own making. Pisceans feel deeply, and as a negative sign can internalise their distress. As a sensitive Water sign, learning to let go of any emotional pain from the past and focusing on the positives of the present will do wonders for their wellbeing. Practising mindfulness through meditation can be a useful tool for a spiritual Piscean to ease their anxieties and bring them back to a present state of calm.

Self-love is important for every sign, but Pisceans can easily forget to nurture themselves whilst they are busy looking after everyone else. Taking time to indulge their creative side can be essential to a Piscean's happiness, but is something they sometimes sacrifice for the sake of others. If a Piscean has an artistic talent, be it with words, art, music, food, or anything else, they should indulge in their creativity and enjoy the healing magic that they can create. Taking time for themselves may have the consequence of having less time for others, which can feel selfish to this giving sign, but taking even an hour to enjoy a bath, read a book, or hone their chosen art is vital for this sign's health and wellbeing. Once a depleted Piscean has been able to recharge their batteries, they will find that they are able to give much more of themselves to the world as a direct result.

Physical activity is a key way for everyone to stay fit, no matter their star sign, but Pisceans can be more interested in stretching their imagination than they are their bodies. If Pisces wants to get into a good exercise routine, finding a sport or physical activity that they enjoy and can be creative in will be important. As a Water sign, Pisces could quite literally be in their element whilst swimming, surfing, or ice skating. If water or an ice rink aren't readily accessible to this sign, their associated body part, feet, could have them dancing their way to fitness in a Zumba class or at their favourite music club. Pisceans will no doubt appreciate the creativity of music and dance and getting healthier will just be a happy bonus for them. Whilst it might be tempting for a Pisces to stick on their best heels before hitting the dancefloor, wearing comfier footwear could save them some plasters and keep their associated body part happy and healthy.

Pisces

....

2020
DIARY PAGES

JANUARY

. . . .

Wednesday 1st

Happy New Year Pisces! The year begins with the Moon in your own sign. Sensitivity about how others perceive you can plague you today. Emotions will be on the edge and you feel misunderstood. This time of the month will always make you dreamier and more disconnected. Try to do something practical.

Thursday 2nd

Today your social circle gets bigger and there is a lot of communication going on. Maybe there are people you have failed to catch up with during the holidays. Now is the time to find others who are on your wavelength and be part of something big and bold.

Friday 3rd

The Moon moves into your sector of money, food and value. Try not to overdo the good things in life today Pisces. Mars is at the last degree of your travel sector and asking you to look back on where you have been and what you have learned recently.

Saturday 4th

Although it is the weekend, your mind may be drawn towards advancement in your career. Your ruler, Mars, has just entered this part of your chart and will add drive and energy to your work. He is a planetary ally and will bring vigour and possibly promotion while he is here.

Sunday 5th

Thinking and speaking may be slow and dull today Pisces. Staying on track in the material world is difficult for you when the Moon enters your communications sector. You will have a tendency to be stubborn and unaccepting when talking to people with widely different views to you. A dinner date can prove productive today.

Monday 6th

The Moon makes a helpful connection to planets in your social sector. It is telling you that this is the area that will cause some unrest for you this year. Use this time to make solid connections with friends and social groups who share your vision Pisces.

Tuesday 7th

Sticking with your social sector, Saturn and Pluto share the same space and discuss power and boundary issues. Pisces, you need to learn who, in your social circle, is exploiting you. Protect your own boundaries now, or your empath qualities may be abused. People will take advantage of your kind soul.

Wednesday 8th

Venus is adding some love and harmony to the discussion going on in your social sector. She is in your sector of dreams and asking you to listen to the lessons you will learn this year but not to give up on your own personal mission. Stay tuned to your spiritual messages too.

Thursday 9th

Family life features today. You may be making a lot of calls or short visits to family members. You can gather information and be the messenger in this area of life. Ensure that this is not gossip or back-stabbing. Laughter can be had now if you allow it.

Friday 10th

The first Full Moon of the year occurs in your creative sector. This is also a lunar eclipse. You will feel nurtured by your creative exploits as they feed your imagination. This sector also deals with love but beware that eclipse: something or someone is hiding in the shadows.

Saturday 11th

Your love life or passion for creativity is getting opposition from the planets in your social sector. There is a need now to balance these two areas. You must make time for friends and your passions or you will feel drained and out of sync with your true purpose.

Sunday 12th

Mercury the messenger joins the planets in your social sector. You must listen hard now. Mercury likes to talk, and when he is next to Saturn and Pluto he may get told off for talking too much. Someone may reveal themselves as a gossip or a liar in your friendship circle.

Monday 13th

The Sun now sits with Saturn and Pluto and is shining his light to make sure that you clearly see what is happening around you. You may need to sort the wheat from the chaff within your social circle. Venus urges you to do this with humanitarian love.

Tuesday 14th

Venus enters your sign today Pisces. She will add love, beauty and harmony to your inner world and it will shine outwards for others to see. People will see you as ethereal and other-worldly. You drift around like a mermaid with Venus here. Try not to drift off too far.

Wednesday 15th

Your attention should be on your significant other or important relationships today, Pisces. The Moon is in this sector and is making a nice connection to your social sector. There is the possibility that your partner is part of your friendship groups or if single, this is where you will find them.

Thursday 16th

Mercury is saying goodbye to your social sector for now. Before he goes, he asks that you be quite sure who your real friends are. Not all are worthy of your time Pisces. Social media contacts can give you a false sense of what friendship is.

Friday 17th

Mercury now enters your dreams and isolation sector. Time alone will become like a superhighway of information in your head. You will think up ideas, dreams and personal quests that excite you. Be careful that you do not spend too much time isolating yourself as Mercury's mind chatter may drive you crazy.

Saturday 18th

You have a desire to travel far and wide. This is key to
transformation for you Pisces. This may be done by higher
education or by joining courses of specific interests. The
occult, esoteric and mystical topics attract you the most
and travelling to exotic places scratches that itch.

Sunday 19th

The Moon in your travel sector connects to the
planets in your social sector. Do you have friends
in foreign lands you could visit? Your online social
groups can be an asset to your thirst for deep and
intense knowledge. It is worth making these contacts
to enhance your learning.

Monday 20th

Emotions and direct action can be blended now as
the Moon sits with Mars in your career sector. As the
Moon also connects to Venus this can be a time for
good relationships between men and women with
both sides seeing the necessity for truth. Equality
rules the workplace.

Tuesday 21st

Your dreamy inner life will be given a boost by the Sun as it enters this sector. Purpose and direction become a part of your vision now. What will be your new mission Pisces? You may fight for a cause under this influence or the cause may be entirely your own.

Wednesday 22nd

Today the Moon enters your busy social sector. For the first time this year, you will feel emotionally attached to your friendship groups. There is some culling to be done here but you are having a hard time doing this. Dropping 'friends' is not in your nature Pisces.

Thursday 23rd

Emotions get bigger today Pisces. You try to do the right thing but forget to put yourself first. There may be some shocks or surprises connected to your dreams sector. It is likely that this will result in an 'aha' moment of enlightenment. This will make you question your self-worth.

Friday 24th

Today there is a New Moon in your dreams sector. This is a great time to make late new year resolutions. Use this time to set intentions for yourself regarding your mission, visions and personal dreams. Men and women will be squaring off today, the workplace will be the battlefield.

Saturday 25th

Mars is lending you his warrior skills in the workplace and you are motivated and driven. If there is an outstanding task or a deadline to meet, today gives you the right energy to get on with it. The power of speech and motivation combined goes a long way today.

Sunday 26th

The Moon in your dreams sector meets Mercury. You now have more reason than ever to take on a mission this year. This is felt deeply in your heart. You have the power to lead others in a rebellion but prefer the quiet way of the spiritual lone warrior.

Monday 27th

An emotional day for you Pisces as the Moon enters your sector dealing with 'self.' Your outward expression may be very sensitive now. With Venus and Neptune sitting together here too, you have a tendency to drift off. Be careful not to self-soothe with substances and keep one foot connected to this planet.

Tuesday 28th

The Moon now meets Neptune in your 'self' sector. This can make your sense of reality a bit twisted. You may not be able to think straight and emotions will wander. Try not to over-think things and get yourself in a more muddled state. Watch for illusions now Pisces.

Wednesday 29th

Your attention is diverted by food and money. These are the tangible things that are needed to bring you back down to earth. Just be careful not to over-indulge as you will regret it later. You want to be forceful at this time but this goes against your delicate nature.

Thursday 30th

Today you will find yourself at a crossroads. This may feel like a dilemma for you. This is just a Moon phase connecting to points concerning the past and the future and will soon pass. At these times the best thing to do is to assess your skill sets to use now.

Friday 31st

There may be issues of control today within your friendship groups. Your sensitive nature picks up on atmospheres but you always feel that they are directed at you. This is not always the case Pisces. Try to stand outside a situation and see it with fresh eyes.

FEBRUARY

. . . .

Saturday 1st

Many small tasks require your attention today Pisces.
This will be a busy weekend. You will feel stubborn and
resentful about the way your time is spent. You may even
have a tantrum. This evening is a great time to indulge in
some good food and company and to relax a little.

Sunday 2nd

Today, Venus will give you a helping hand in getting
what you want. Friendship groups may try to manipulate
you, but you will have the upper hand. Simply be your
kind and generous self and you will find that you have
a joyous day with friends and groups. Build on good
connections now.

Monday 3rd

Mercury is at the very last degree of your entire chart.
Listen carefully to your inner self as this is Mercury
discussing his new mission with you. Dreams and
visions are about to become a reality. Take this seriously
and make this year the foundation for a new you.

Tuesday 4th

The Moon in your family sector brings a lot of networking your way. Talking and laughing with family members means a lot. You may have to make some short trips to see people but friendly, happy chatter makes this a pleasure. Mercury is at the starting block ready for you.

Wednesday 5th

Actions and emotions may be at odds today Pisces. Watch out for irritability in the workplace which is in direct conflict with your family obligations. Home life is where you are emotionally invested but work is making demands on you today. Friends can show where your selflessness can be a problem.

Thursday 6th

The Moon is at a point in the sky that is connected to your destiny. This happens in your creative and love sector. Your heart will take a leap into the future and draw you towards projects that are nurturing. You need a cause or quest that brings fulfilment.

Friday 7th

Venus is now at the last degree of your 'self' sector. You are allowed to be indulgent today Pisces. Good food, good company and some loving with a special person will honour Venus. Her lessons on self-worth will stand you in good stead for the rest of the year.

Saturday 8th

The Moon makes its way into your health and duties sector. Here you can shine and be expressive. Putting your mind to mundane chores and being of service to others is good for you. Venus becomes the Warrior Goddess in your money house now. Time to be vigilant with your spending.

Sunday 9th

A Full Moon occurs in your duties sector. This will highlight how you stand out from the crowd with your willingness to go the extra mile. You may find that something has come to completion now. This might be a project or a task where you have shown leadership qualities and self-expression.

Monday 10th

As the Moon moves into your relationship sector, important people in your life come into focus. Relating will be better for you if you succeed in paying attention to the small details. The Pisces need to merge works better in significant relationships if you can learn to be a little more grounded.

Tuesday 11th

Today brings an easy connection between lovers and friends. The big planets in your social sector will be teaching you a thing or two about how you can manage your love relationships and friendships. Boundaries, ethics and control will be your keywords for this year. Listen to your lover.

Wednesday 12th

How does a Pisces deal with the deeper mysteries of life? The Moon is in your sector of sex, death and rebirth and you can get lost in the darkness here. You require peace and harmony which conflicts with your need to drift freely. You are a slippery fish Pisces.

Thursday 13th

Today you will feel out of sorts with your social sector. You have a lot of acquaintances who simply do not understand the deeper you. However, you have close friends who are always there for you. You find yourself torn between the old and the new.

Friday 14th

This can be an intense day with deep feelings that you cannot grasp. You can deal with this best by doing some research or travel. Esoteric and occult subjects can lead you to foreign lands and keep you interested. Discuss this possibility with a partner today and you may find that a big adventure beckons.

Saturday 15th

Mercury is soon to go retrograde so use the weekend to back up devices. Make sure that travel plans are double-checked and refrain from signing anything over the next three weeks. This will happen in your own sign so you may feel a little victimised now poor Pisces.

Sunday 16th

Mars has left your career sector and joins the other planets in your social sector. Unfortunately, this can be a time of hostility between friendship groups. You can be driven and forceful now but there is a chance of bullying. Ensure that you are not the bully Pisces.

Monday 17th

Mercury retrograde begins. Get your head down and deal with your day to day job today Pisces. You achieve emotional satisfaction from a job well done. Your mind may wander and you seek a broader perspective in your career. Is there a possibility of working abroad or higher education concerning your career?

Tuesday 18th

You may see some truth behind an illusion you have been fostering. Jupiter connects to Neptune in your sign making illusions bigger or dispelling the fog and seeing the truth. Where have you been deceived Pisces? Have you been deceiving yourself? Social groups will be involved in this revelation today.

Wednesday 19th

The Sun now enters your sign which means that it is
your birthday month Pisces. The deep waters that you
swim around in will become warmer now. You will have
the chance to express yourself beautifully and creatively
whilst the Sun is here. This is your time to laugh and play.

Thursday 20th

The Moon makes its monthly visit to your social sector
and will meet each of the planets there. This time of
the month can be turbulent and emotions will vacillate
quickly. Remember that this is just a passing Moon phase
and will be over by the day's end. Stick with it Pisces.

Friday 21st

Mars the planet of war and Uranus the planet of
disruption are connecting today. This is a positive
connection so expect a surprise or some enlightenment.
Your social sector and communications sector will reveal
a possible rebellion or new cause for you to back. You
hate discrimination now.

Saturday 22nd

The Moon in your dreams and isolation sector adds
to the surprise from yesterday. The Sun in your sign is
also connecting to Uranus so this will not be a shock
but some good news and will make you happy and
emotional. Time alone will help you process this.

Sunday 23rd

You have a New Moon in your sign today Pisces. This is a chance to set good intentions and make affirmations regarding your own being and how you present yourself to others. Do you remember that new mission that Mercury whispered in your ear? Now is time to plant that seed in reality.

Monday 24th

Venus, the planet of love, money, food and harmony is squaring off to Jupiter today. He is in your social sector and this may mean that Venus' influence is making you selfish. This could rub people up the wrong way but it is a good lesson in boundaries Pisces.

Tuesday 25th

You will be irritable today as thoughts of the past come back to you. There are things that you would like to have done but did not. Thinking about this brings regrets and resentment. You feel that you have not achieved what you desire. This is foolish, you have a new mission now.

Wednesday 26th

Mercury has nothing to say today as he is in the heart of the Sun. Remember that he is retrograde in your sign. Today you will be thinking and remaining quiet. Keep your thoughts to yourself today. Plans are forming but you are not yet ready to reveal them.

Thursday 27th

Be careful that you do not overspend or over-eat today.
You will be impulsive and can make rash decisions
concerning money. You may want to use that energy to
change your home around or do something practical
instead. Physical exercise is a good way to do this.

Friday 28th

You feel more stable today. Plans come out of your head
and down onto paper. Set your mind to a task list and
work your way through it. This may include short trips
or phone calls. When that list is all ticked off you may
enjoy a treat. Dinner for one maybe?

Saturday 29th

Mercury has found his voice again and is chatting to
Uranus who turns everything into a radical new idea.
You will surprise yourself at the innovations coming
out of your head Pisces. Beware of control issues today,
someone may want to jump on your bandwagon and
steal your glory.

MARCH
· · · · · · · · · · · · · ·

Sunday 1st

A stable, earthy Moon lends a sensible approach to
the planets in your social sector. Communication with
friends will be solid and dependable. You may begin to
work out who are your allies and who are the people
taking advantage of you. Friends you have had for many
years stand out as the true ones.

Monday 2nd

Family chatter will fill your head now. Everyone knows
each other's business and all are eager to voice their
opinion. Remember to think before you speak as Mercury
is still in retrograde and can cause havoc in situations like
this. Mind your own business right now Pisces.

Tuesday 3rd

The Moon in your family sector each month will mean
that you may become the family sounding board.
Members may bitch about each other and you are called
upon for empathy. This can be an area where you are
drained Pisces. You must strengthen your boundaries or
learn to stay impartial.

Wednesday 4th

Today you may nurture yourself by doing something artistic. This is easy for you Pisces as you are the poet of the zodiac. Creative expression is food for your soul. You are sensitive now. You may feel a little troubled in your inner world and want to isolate yourself.

Thursday 5th

Venus moves into her own sign and starts to build her empire. For you, Pisces, this means that your communication sector will have more harmony and balance. There will be a conflict between mothers and fathers or other role models today. Your drive to succeed is opposing your creative freedom.

Friday 6th

You will feel restricted today and your creativity or self-expression will suffer. This may also be a problem in a love affair where one person is trying to exert control. Something is asking to be transformed now Pisces. Do you know what it is?

Saturday 7th

Find the joy in anything you do today Pisces. From being of service to mundane chores, there is something to make you smile. People look to you to be a ray of sunshine who can motivate others. Check in with your health today and make sure that you laugh. Be childlike and have some fun.

Sunday 8th

Today will feel surreal and dreamy. Conversations may be a mix of love and rebellion. There will be a feeling of fog around you which is being burned away. You may change your perspective about yourself now Pisces. A startling revelation can dissolve an outworn belief about yourself. This is good.

Monday 9th

A Full Moon in your relationship sector will illuminate where you may have been a martyr. You must learn the difference between willing service and unnecessary sacrifice. There is a chance that you have been duped and you are seeing this now. What has been building for the last six months?

Tuesday 10th

Mercury goes direct again today. He will retrace his steps once more and get you back on track with your personal mission. Listen well to teachers and gurus. Do your research and gather information for your quest. When Mercury returns to your sign you must be ready to go.

Wednesday 11th

Emotions need to be balanced now and you can do this by understanding that every ending has a new beginning that follows it. Learning about the cycles of death and rebirth will help you deal with loss. This is making space for something new to emerge so embrace this Pisces.

Thursday 12th

An intense Moon enters your travel sector and you may start jotting down notes for your mission. The exotic, erotic and exciting attract you now. This is part of your research and can take you to faraway lands even if only in your mind. Enjoy this kind of travelling for now Pisces.

Friday 13th

This is a nice day to get in touch with your body Pisces. An ethereal creature like you needs to ground sometimes and today the planetary connections are favourable. Take a walk in nature, do yoga, have sex or eat a delicious meal. Tantalise your senses and feel connected.

Saturday 14th

You will feel that familiar nagging to help a friend in need today. Unfortunately, you fail to see where you are being manipulated. You are a soft touch Pisces and you may come across someone who is passive aggressive towards you today. Think before responding. How does this serve you?

Sunday 15th

Mercury is again at the last degree of your entire chart. This is the deepest, most secret part of you and you may not even recognise yourself here. This is a tipping point. Do you take the challenge of a new mission or do you miss out on an adventure?

Monday 16th

Now Mercury enters the deep waters of your sign. The urge to connect deeply with everyone is the nature of your new mission. There are some who can use and abuse you. Your mission is to swim around and assess your connections with people. They must be built on solid ground.

Tuesday 17th

You will feel uncertain for the next week. This is normal at the beginning of a new mission so go with the feelings and see what comes up for you. You may feel like you are on an impossible hero's quest but you, of all signs, will see it through to the end.

53

Wednesday 18th

Emotions will be unsettled today. You will doubt
yourself. Be happy about yourself and feel that you
need to take back some control. Let these feelings pass
as quickly as they came. Friends from different areas
will give you varied responses today. This can muddle
your thinking.

Thursday 19th

The Moon moves into your dream sector and you want to
be alone. You have new thoughts and perspectives that you
need to process. This is best done alone as your radical
thinking may cause others to question you. Get lost in your
thoughts but come back to the shore when ready.

Friday 20th

It is the Spring Equinox today and you have another
chance to set goals and intentions. At this time of
balance, the Sun has just entered your money and value
sector. It would be beneficial if you could resolve to
bring balance to that area of your life.

Saturday 21st

The Moon enters your sign and meets up with Mercury.
You may have an emotional heart to heart with someone
today. Speak your mind Pisces, as you do not often
get the chance. Let someone know how you feel, your
concerns and how to treat you. Stand up for yourself.

CONTENTS

Sunday 22nd

Saturn makes a big shift into your dreams sector. This will mark the next two and a half years as a lesson in how you spend your time alone. You will learn about choosing causes wisely and not wasting your time on anything that drains your naturally empathic soul.

Monday 23rd

Today you will feel extra emotional or dreamy and may even cut yourself off and have some alone time. This would be a good thing to do as your social circle will be having some power and control issues now. Stay out of it and enjoy a little dream of your own, Pisces.

Tuesday 24th

A New Moon in your money and resources sector urges you to look at how you value yourself Pisces. This will be a year where you will learn how to put yourself first. Anything begun now will have a great chance of being completed. What will it be Pisces?

Wednesday 25th

After the stillness of the Equinox and the New Moon, you may feel eager to start new projects or carry out new plans. Use this time to do a little research and be sure of your goals for the next twelve months. Look back at what has worked before.

Thursday 26th

Today can feel overwhelming but be assured that it is not just you Pisces. The Moon in your communications sector is sitting with Uranus the disruptor and making bad connections to almost every other planet. Sit tight and keep your head down. There will be restless energy in all areas.

Friday 27th

You may want to begin the weekend with an evening out with friends. Conversations over good food and wine are favoured for an enjoyable evening. Pick the right friends to dine with as you will be stubborn or bullish with the wrong ones Pisces. Lifelong friends will be supportive.

Saturday 28th

Whatever you do today will be done with a lot of love. Venus is in your communications sector making a great connection with Jupiter in your social sector. Love, peace and harmony will surround you now. Jupiter enlarges what he touches. This is a very joyful day for you and your friends Pisces.

Sunday 29th

This is a family day filled with chats and laughter. Siblings feature highly today. Family is a good place for you to sound off and brainstorm ideas for new plans. Family members have sound advice for you based on their experiences. Take it all in.

Monday 30th

Mars is at the last degree of your social sector. There will be a lot happening there this year and so he asks you quite aggressively to check that you have the right people around you. Your energy and drive can depend on who is demanding your attention here.

Tuesday 31st

Mars meets Saturn as he enters your dreams sector. You will slow down today and listen to your elders. Bosses or patriarchal figures will have something to teach you about your dreams and visions. There will also be something to learn about how you overdo self-sacrifice or make decisions without thinking.

APRIL
....

Wednesday 1st

Today is a dreamy, floaty sort of day which you will love Pisces. You have a lot of creative energy flooding your mind today. This is great for those of you who are poets or artists as you will feel in tune with the spiritual world and your own inner world.

Thursday 2nd

Check in with your health today. Usually, you can be a very strong person, inside and out but your mundane chores may be getting on top of you. Your leadership qualities are evident today in the way you apply yourself to any task that you are given.

Friday 3rd

Venus enters your family sector. She will inject some love and harmony into this area of your life. You can evaluate your self-worth while she is here. Assess if this is another area where your good nature is being taken for granted. Share the love Pisces.

Saturday 4th

Today is another day where you stop and think about your role within groups. Are you doing enough of what you desire Pisces? Is there enough time for you in your daily life? Mercury is passing his mission statement to Neptune whose influence can make you switch off or self-sacrifice.

Sunday 5th

Two planets in your social sector meet up today. Jupiter teaches about law and justice while Pluto wants transformation or control. Any issues that you come across today may be out of proportion so sit tight and let this influence pass before acting on anything you perceive to be unfair.

Monday 6th

The Moon in your relationship sector adds emotions to the Jupiter and Pluto meet-up. You may feel criticised or belittled by a partner. You will need to ensure that there is enough time on your schedule for both friends and lovers. Maybe your lover is in your friendship group.

Tuesday 7th

There are some surprises or shocks today. You will be asserting yourself and trying to make people understand how unique you are. Not everyone shares your vision Pisces. It will be difficult to find a balance today between your own ideals and those of others. This may involve a loved one.

Wednesday 8th

A Full Moon occurs in your sector of sex, death and rebirth Pisces. This will illuminate anything you have been working on for the last six months. You may find that someone is not on your wavelength and issues that are important to you are not so to them.

Thursday 9th

As the Moon enters your travel sector, your deeper philosophies concern you. You will find it hard to reconcile your beliefs now and you argue with others. Tempers can flare and upset people. You will need to think outside the box today and accept that there are other truths.

Friday 10th

The Moon makes a connection with the planets in your social sector. You call on old friends or trusted interest groups to help validate the beliefs you are struggling with. You begin to see another point of view and transform some of your views. You are able to adapt to this.

Saturday 11th

Mercury now enters your money and value sector. This sector also deals with food and will be a good day to enjoy good conversation over a nice meal. Father figures or bosses may be involved here too. You will learn something to your advantage today Pisces.

Sunday 12th

Right now, you feel that it is the right time to speak up about your new plans. You have many ideas to share with people but your deeper mission is to build healthy boundaries. This comes back to your mind today and there are one or two people you can discuss this with.

Monday 13th

Once again, friendships and social groups are taking up most of your mind space. Think about who you are dependent on. Think about who depends on you. Are your relationships with friends mutually satisfying Pisces? How far will you go before you see that some are just not worth your efforts?

Tuesday 14th

Control issues will surface today Pisces. These will play on your mind and cut you deeply. Old wounds may come back to be healed. How can you transform your wounds with love? If this is you trying to control something then forget it, it is not going to work.

Wednesday 15th

Be careful today as there is a possibility that you may over-spend or over-eat. Neither of these things is good for you Pisces and your stomach or your bank balance will suffer greatly. On the other hand, there could be a great celebration to which you are invited.

Thursday 16th

Your dreams and visions will be supported by your family life today. You may connect with a family member in a different way as they will encourage you to live your dreams and carry out your mission of establishing boundaries. Perhaps they have experience with this issue. A family trait maybe?

Friday 17th

The Moon now dips into your sign and you can be moody, broody or away with the fairies. People close to you understand that you can sometimes seem to be on a different planet but today there may be others who ridicule your ways of understanding the world around you.

Saturday 18th

There will be some sweet-talking going on in your family sector today. Members may rally around and want your company. Make sure that this is for the right reasons. Always put your self-worth above anything you are asked to do by anyone, family included.

Sunday 19th

Today you are more assertive than you have been for some time. Mars in your dreams sector gives you the drive and the energy to bring your dreams and wishes closer to manifestation. The Sun moves into your communications sector and you will notice that you are taken more seriously over the next month.

Monday 20th

The Moon shifts and adds to the positive, forward-moving energy. You will be taking a good look into the future and fitting your mission into your daily life. If this does not work out, you will find a way of making your mission your daily life instead.

Tuesday 21st

Relationships between men and women go well today. There is a nice balance between family interactions and alone time. Someone may try to rock the boat but they will not get very far. On the whole, the day pans out nicely for you Pisces. You will come out a winner today.

Wednesday 22nd

You will have to put your foot down today Pisces. You or someone around you is acting in a very stubborn way. There will be some sulking or temper tantrums. Male role models will need to step up and have a few words with the offender.

Thursday 23rd

Today, a New Moon in your communications sector can help you to make mini resolutions about how you converse with people. Short trips and siblings can be on your list of things to do and people to see. Research projects will get a boost now and can be built on solid ground.

Friday 24th

You may get a short, sharp shock today when the Moon passes Uranus in your communications sector. This may also come as an 'aha' moment and be the catalyst you need to get your New Moon intention activated. You may throw your hands up in the air and shout "Why me?"

Saturday 25th

Mercury and Pluto are squaring off today and you find that there is a conflict of interests between money and friends. Do not let anyone try to control how you manage your finances. This may be a trip organised with a social group and will require you to pay out.

Sunday 26th

Pluto, the planet that deals with power and control, is the first of the planets in your social sector to retrograde. You will find that the next few months will be the testing ground for your 2020 mission. Today's planetary energy asks you to stay indoors and speak to no-one.

Monday 27th

A nurturing Moon in your creative sector settles your anxiety. This is also the area concerned with falling in love Pisces. However, knowing you, you find a new artist or writer to fall in love with. Mercury enters your communication sector and will chat the next few weeks away.

Tuesday 28th

Today you have a deep yearning in your heart to be somewhere else. Passionate feelings will be laced with a hint of melancholy. This is typical Pisces stuff so swim with it and create some of your best art or writing. Love will be highlighted and favoured now under this influence.

Wednesday 29th

Heartfelt longing seems to turn against you today and you feel fated to miss out on love. This is not the case Pisces. This is a passing Moon phase opposing Jupiter who is increasing your mood and newly retrograde Pluto who does not like being unable to control things.

Thursday 30th

As the Moon shifts, so does your mood. You now shine brightly and your self-expression puts you at centre stage. People look up to you now. The danger here is that you might inflate your ego too much and become obnoxious. Nobody likes a show-off Pisces. Lead from your heart.

MAY

....

Friday 1st
Volatile and hostile behaviour surrounds you today
Pisces. You feel that you are being pursued by idiots.
There is a chance that running around doing everything
for everyone will bring you to tipping point and you
may be the one to explode. Arguments are likely under
this unstable influence.

Saturday 2nd
You need a quiet day. This a great time to check in with
a special person, or if you are single, to check in with
your inner lover and spoil yourself. If you are still feeling
tense and irritable, you may need to look at your own
shadow now. How are you projecting yourself Pisces?

Sunday 3rd
Important relationships will soothe you today. You feel
back in control of your emotions. Sweet conversations
over dinner or intimate time will help you see that
there is someone out there who is willing to share
your load. Politeness and good behaviour go in your
favour now Pisces.

Monday 4th

Mercury sits in the heart of the Sun and receives new information for you. This time could feel fuzzy for you and you may be unable to communicate properly, but wait until Mercury shifts. This phase will not last long. You try to reconcile the mysteries of life with your own philosophies today.

Tuesday 5th

The point in the sky that is concerned with fate and destiny moves into your family sector. The next eighteen months will be about how you share and receive information within your family setting. You may even be thinking of a family of your own or your ancestry now.

Wednesday 6th

Travel may well be on your mind today Pisces. Exotic places call you. Ancient religions or a search for truth will be on your bucket list now. You are soul-searching now and you believe that you will find answers in foreign lands and cultures. This can be an intense time.

Thursday 7th

The Full Moon in your travel sector today adds to the intensity of your mood. It has you questioning your belief systems. Occult or esoteric topics interest you now. If you have learned anything like this over the last six months, what is it that is now jumping out at you?

Friday 8th

The Moon hits a point that is looking back at the past.
What skill set have you brought with you into the
present? What have you learned in the past which may
become useful once more? Higher education courses
from days gone by may attract you again now.

Saturday 9th

Mercury is connecting to Pluto today and asking how
you are in control of your money, your home life and
your resources. There is something around you that can
be transformed and be made beautiful. How are you
at buying and selling Pisces? Recycling old clothes or
furniture may become a project for you.

Sunday 10th

Now Mercury connects to Jupiter. You recall an
inspirational teacher from your past. This can be an
actual teacher or someone who brought you great joy
and wisdom. Is there anyone like that in your life now
Pisces? There may be someone coming in to fill that role.

Monday 11th

Saturn now goes retrograde. He is going to retrace his
steps in your social sector and get you looking at those
boundaries of yours. This is a major lesson for you this
year. Saturn's lessons are hard and if you do not learn
them, they will come back again and again.

Tuesday 12th

Mercury has left your communications sector and now flies into your family sector. There is already a lot of conversation here but expect more over the next two weeks. A family get together is possible, during which there is a lot of laughter. Mercury also brings his bag of tricks.

Wednesday 13th

Venus goes retrograde in your family sector. This will take forty days and can cause a lot of unrest if Mercury lets her get away with it. Look out for upsets regarding mother figures or wives and female partners. A long lost family member could reappear now.

Thursday 14th

While Venus was turning around yesterday, Mars moved into your own sign Pisces. This may mean that you become aggressive or very direct. Taking up an exercise regime of some sort can help to use Mars' energy the right way. Watch out for passive-aggressive behaviour while Mars is here.

Friday 15th

Now Jupiter also turns retrograde. Again, this happens
in your social sector. You were warned that this is
the area which will need the most attention this year.
Jupiter can squeeze out any joy and optimism at this
time, but fear not, his lesson is there to help you grow,
and Jupiter likes growth.

Saturday 16th

Today you will feel the first effects of the Venus
retrograde. The Moon is in your sign and making a bad
connection to Venus in your family sector. You may be
put upon or scapegoated. People will be demanding
your time and energy. This will not go down well.

Sunday 17th

The Moon shifts and you will feel more assertive.
Standing up for yourself now is crucial as you need to
set a standard. Let people know what you will and will
not tolerate. You must dig your heels in and refuse to
move from this standpoint.

Monday 18th

Self-expression comes easier today. If the message has
not been received by people who are using you, Mercury
lends you his power of speech. You can say what is on
your mind and in your heart. This will probably upset a
few people but it is for your own good Pisces.

Tuesday 19th

Things are a little smoother today. The Moon connects with Venus and you may even get an apology or two. You can get your own way now but not in a pushy way. Venus will do this with love. Your desires and wishes are important too, people need to know that.

Wednesday 20th

The Sun now enters your family sector. This will either heat up any unrest or cause some burn-out within the current tension. You realise that all the fuss was for nothing. You can be more stubborn with the Moon in your communications sector but you must make a stand.

Thursday 21st

There is a feeling of some sort of closure now. Skeletons may have come out of the family closet or dirty washing has been aired in public. You must draw a line under a recent argument. Healing can take place now that this is out in the open Pisces.

Friday 22nd

Today there is a New Moon in your family sector. Although there is still some time to go with Venus retrograding there, now is your chance to make personal affirmations regarding how to deal with similar situations in the future. Learn to respond and not to react. Think before you speak.

Saturday 23rd

Tension is still in the air as the Moon connects uneasily to Mars. Emotion is in conflict with your natural desires and urges. You are still angry and feel that you have not said your piece. Let it go Pisces. Use that pent-up energy to exercise.

Sunday 24th

The Moon touches that point of fate for the first time since it has changed signs. You will feel extra emotional and determined to see some changes made. Think about doing a new course of study which may help you towards your personal mission or career prospects.

Monday 25th

Now is the time to put your soulful mood into something creative. Once more this is the time for poets and artists to express themselves. You may also confide in a love interest and turn this into a romantic day. You can nurture yourself this way Pisces. Put your feelings to paper.

Tuesday 26th

A Moon and Pluto opposition means that today you can experience a battle of wills with someone. Do not let anyone else dictate how you feel. This energy is also good for transforming an old project into a new one. Is there something hidden under the stairs that you can do this with?

Wednesday 27th

Today, you would benefit most by getting on with everyday jobs and checking your 'to do' list. You will gain satisfaction by working methodically through your tasks with a smile on your face. Health and fitness will also benefit from check-ups or an overdue visit to the gym.

Thursday 28th

Mercury says goodbye to your family sector and jumps nimbly into your creative sector. Mothering roles can play a part now and small children can lighten the room with their laughter. Caring for someone or something you are passionate about now will help distract you from any tension around you.

Friday 29th

The weekend starts with the Moon in your
relationship sector. It would be good for you to think
about your loved one's needs. You can self-partner
now if you are single. Take yourself on a date or cook
an extra special favourite meal.

Saturday 30th

Your important relationships are where you feel you
can compromise. To you Pisces, an equal partnership
means that you are willing to go the extra mile for your
loved one. Remember, you do not have to do this for
everyone in your life.

Sunday 31st

You will try to balance out the superficial with the deep
and meaningful today. This is not possible and you
will need to change the way you think about this. The
Moon in your sector of sex, death and rebirth makes you
wonder why so many concepts are out of your reach.

JUNE
·················

Monday 1st
June begins with you taking a long hard look at what
your themes for the year are. It is already half-way
through 2020. You have realised by now that the major
lessons for you are concerned with friendships and
social circles. This also includes online media. Take a
breather and gather your strength.

Tuesday 2nd
There will be significant unrest between men and
women today. Venus and Mars are squaring off and
of course, Venus is in retrograde. Information may be
withheld in your family sector. Venus can be stubborn
or bitchy today whilst Mars is swimming against the
tide in your sign.

Wednesday 3rd
Today you will experience a stalemate situation as Venus
is in the heart of the Sun and has gone AWOL. She will
not listen so there is no point in forcing an issue now.
This is likely to cause an explosion or temper tantrum as
there are things that need to be said.

Thursday 4th

Tension is building so the best thing you can do today is to get your head down at work. You can make some headway with your goals and deadlines as there is a fiery Moon, which helps your motivation. You may feel like forgetting everything and riding off into the sunset.

Friday 5th

Today there is a Full Moon in your career sector. Something will come to a head now. What have you been working on for the last six months, Pisces? You desire freedom and new experiences. Is it possible to travel with your work? Talk to the boss today.

Saturday 6th

Consider how far you have come Pisces. What have you been building or progressing towards? Baby steps are all it takes to climb a mountain. Think about new goals and evaluate which ones did not work out for you. Maybe it is time to let those go now.

Sunday 7th

The Moon is in your social sector. Spend some time with friends or your online connections. Social media groups can be fulfilling today. Make sure that your mission to sort out real friends from users includes your online connections. Do not take on too many leadership roles now.

Monday 8th

Retrograde planets in your social sector get hit today
by the emotional Moon. When things go wrong you feel
them deeply and personally and this is more intense this
year. Pluto is asking you to make changes or cuts. Jupiter
is looking for justice and joy. Which friendships need to
be transformed?

Tuesday 9th

The Moon slips into the deepest part of your chart and
you feel like being alone or raising a revolution. Saturn
is here to teach you how to respect and value your alone
time. This is not the time to wallow in self-pity with
drugs or alcohol.

Wednesday 10th

The Sun in your family sector is connecting to Neptune
in your own sign. You feel unclear and muddled today.
Neptune dissolves things, especially the boundaries
that Saturn is asking you to build. This could be a
difficult day for you but hang in there, this will pass
quickly. Do not fret.

Thursday 11th

Today you are feeling extra sorry for yourself but there is great news Pisces. You are a master poet and artist. Use those skills to express your melancholy mood. This energy can make you a damsel in distress or a knight without a quest. Express it Pisces, it will be useful.

Friday 12th

You struggle a little today. Family are again making demands on you. There is only so much you can do for someone before you compromise yourself. Stay on track with your mission and very gently, say no. This might upset some people but will make you stronger for the future.

Saturday 13th

There is crazy energy today as the Moon crosses Mars then Neptune. This occurs in your sector of 'self', Pisces. Your mood may swing back and forth between aggression and compliance. Try not to be passive-aggressive. Maybe it is best if you have the day to yourself and avoid people.

Sunday 14th

Your mood picks up and you are more assertive. Energy
levels are getting higher and you are able to move
through the day getting things done. Working through
a 'to-do' list will bring you satisfaction. New ideas and
ways of doing things connected with your resources will
surface today.

Monday 15th

You are just not feeling it today Pisces. This is one of
those days where your words just do not come out right.
You feel misunderstood today or your new ideas may
have to be scrapped as they are just not working out. Try
not to have important meetings today.

Tuesday 16th

You regain your balance and can think straight again.
The Moon moves into your communications sector and
heartfelt conversations with family are on the agenda.
Mercury is soon to go retrograde again so speak up now.
Good company and food will make the day a winner.
Make sure everyone is on the same page.

Wednesday 17th

The energy today is like waiting to start a race. Do not worry Pisces, you will not be doing any running. You may be busy making a lot of short trips or catching up on emails and phone calls. There is anticipation in the air. Try to find some time to ground yourself.

Thursday 18th

Mercury retrograde begins. The little trickster will be attempting to cause havoc in your creative sector. This is also the area that deals with falling in love. You wish to feel nurtured and fulfilled now but be warned that Mercury will lull you into a false sense of security.

Friday 19th

You desire to make some sort of change today. This could be as simple as a haircut or re-organising your home. There is not a lot that you are in control of at this time so make small changes and feel your way into any big one you deem necessary.

Saturday 20th

As the Summer Solstice approaches, your energy levels rise. This is a good time to start a new fitness regime or a healthy diet. You will go for this in a big way. Dreams may be more vivid now. Listen to them, they are telling you something important Pisces.

Sunday 21st

Today there is a New Moon and an eclipse on the longest day of the year. You may make some powerful affirmations now but there is a dark side to this. The eclipse throws its shadow over the longest day of the year. This is a warning to be on guard.

Monday 22nd

The Moon makes its way through your creative sector and makes you more needy than usual. Mother figures can feature today and you have a desire for comfort foods and security. Being with someone you feel strongly about is possibly the best thing you can do today Pisces.

Tuesday 23rd

Another of the outer planets goes retrograde today. Neptune, the planet connected with dreams and dissolving things turns around in its own sign of Pisces. This is going to make it far more difficult to put boundaries in place. Anything you have built recently may fall apart.

Wednesday 24th

You may not feel as strong as you usually do now Pisces. This would be a good time to get a health check-up or review your fitness and eating habits. Daily routines may drain your energy now. Make sure that you have enough free time for yourself to kick back and relax.

Thursday 25th

Venus retrograde is over. You can now review what this time has meant for you. There may have been break-ups, make-ups or someone from the past returning but these are all lessons. The Moon in your opposite sign of Virgo will give you a hint about relationships.

Friday 26th

Your poor energy levels are pulled two ways today Pisces. There are many dreams and visions that you would like to manifest but they seem impossible. You fall back on old habits and forget about trying something new. Stay in that space until the Moon passes and you can move forward.

Saturday 27th

Mars is responsible for your energy and drive. He is now at the last degree of your sign and is eager to get going in his own sign. However, it is important now that you take a break before charging in on something new. Today there is a conflict between you and another.

Sunday 28th

Mars is finally in his own sign. This is your sector of money and value Pisces. Does Mars want you to go mad spending a lot of money? You will need to rein in your impulses while he is here as this could get you, your bank balance and your waistline into trouble.

Monday 29th

Today is a very difficult day. The Moon is in your relationship sector and is squaring off to each of the retrograde planets in your social sector. You will be torn between your lover and your friendships. Your shadow-side may surface and you will be projecting your mood onto others.

Tuesday 30th

Jupiter and Pluto are sitting together and discussing how control issues need to be transformed. Anything along these lines will be felt intensely today. Jupiter wants you to see the truth behind some of the connections that you place value in. Are they worth it Pisces?

JULY

. . . .

Wednesday 1st

Mercury has nothing to say today. He is receiving new
information for your creative or love pursuits. Your
mind may be overloaded with creativity bursting to
get out but you do not know where to start. Mercury's
influence may also mean that you are listening more.
Good for you Pisces.

Thursday 2nd

Saturn has returned to your social sector and you must
sit up and take note. What goes on at this time will be
a major lesson in setting personal boundaries. You will
now see who is taking advantage of you and who truly
wants to spend time with you.

Friday 3rd

Career is foremost in your mind today. You have a need
to grow away from a possibly stagnant work situation.
Travel or higher education can help you advance in
your career. Now is a good time to think about this. Your
energy and aspirations are high today. Aim high.

Saturday 4th

The Moon now enters your troublesome social sector.
You will feel something building with anticipation in
this area. Are there any friendships or connections that
are holding you back from achieving your potential?
Is there a new group you would like to join? You are
restless and aware of the need for change.

Sunday 5th

Today there is a Full Moon and a lunar eclipse in your
social sector. Hopefully, this will illuminate the changes
you need to make here. However, the shadow of the
eclipse is a warning. Either you are not yet prepared to
transform this area of your life, or you do not have all
the information you need.

Monday 6th

Dream away, Pisces. The energy today is just perfect for
a little relaxation and self-indulgence. You can connect
to God or Spirit easily now. You may allow your mind
to wander into your hopes and wishes for the future.
Family members may be helpful and supportive.

Tuesday 7th

There is some very positive energy available to you
today. What are you going to do with it? You may
find that you are having some innovative and genius
thoughts and would like to put them into practice. Why
not brainstorm the idea with friends first?

Wednesday 8th

Mars and Mercury are at odds today. This is never a good sign when Mercury is in retrograde. You must be vigilant as this energy can cause carelessness and accidents of all kinds. People can be pig-headed and aggressive now. Watch that your words do not hurt someone. Think before you speak and act.

Thursday 9th

The Moon is in your sign and making an uneasy connection to Venus. Family members may request your presence for favours. You want to do your own thing today however and have no time for others. This will cause some upset but is necessary for your growth this year Pisces.

Friday 10th

Having some alone time will do you good today. You can be rather melancholic and difficult for others to deal with. This is absolutely fine Pisces. Stay home, treat yourself to something you enjoy and have fun in your own little world of dreams. Write poetry, make art, express yourself.

Saturday 11th

Today you lift yourself out of isolation and connect
more. This may be a shopping trip or a dinner date.
Either way, try not to over-indulge with food or money.
You will feel more like going after what you want today
and can be selfish but in a good way.

Sunday 12th

Mercury goes direct today. You can get back on track
with your creative goals. Any love interests can now be
pursued without fear of being misunderstood. The Sun
is making a nice connection to Neptune in your sign
and you see a situation clearly now. Neptune's mist has
been burned away.

Monday 13th

As the Moon enters your communication sector, you will
be more determined to say your piece. There is a topic
that you feel strongly about and will not change your
opinion or see another point of view. Make sure that you
base this on solid evidence and stand your ground.

Tuesday 14th

Today your stubbornness in conversations can cause an
argument. Uranus, the planet of disruption, is tagged
by the Moon and you may feel that someone is trying to
antagonise you on purpose. Do not rise to it Pisces. The
Sun exposes a bully or liar in your social circle.

Wednesday 15th

The Sun is your friend right now as he now gives you more insight into the troublemakers in your friendship groups. This time he is opposite Pluto and showing you who is trying to manipulate and control you. You get a better idea of what needs to change now.

Thursday 16th

The Moon slips into your family sector and grants you a fun time. You are nurtured by your family as they, or most of them, speak your language. They understand you better than most people. There will be no control issues from this area today. Enjoy your family time Pisces.

Friday 17th

The Moon and Venus meet up and have a ladies' night. This adds harmony and heartfelt emotion to your family sector. Mothers and females in general feature highly under this influence. Conversations flow freely and ideas are shared. You may be philosophising or enjoying the company of a loved one tonight.

Saturday 18th

The safety and security of a loving family are crucial to you, Pisces. The Moon dips into your creative and love sector and you are awash with comfortable feelings. A lover may fit into your family very well. Alternatively, your lover's family may feel like your own. Happy days Pisces.

Sunday 19th

Today can be filled with love and merry laughter. The
Moon meets Mercury and has a head and heart talk.
You do not hold your feelings back at this time but
you must remember your mission. Not only must you
safeguard your own boundaries but you must respect
those of others too.

Monday 20th

There is a gorgeous New Moon in your creative
sector today Pisces. You have had a lovely few days of
optimism and unconditional love around you. This
Moon asks you to set affirmations based on loving,
nurturing and protecting. The Sun will help you with a
boundaries issue today.

Tuesday 21st

Be courageous Pisces. Today you are asked to lead by
example. Lead from a place of love and strength. Show
the compassionate person you are but keep your mission
in mind. Do not be a pushover. If you are tested by
someone, stay strong and say no, thank you.

Wednesday 22nd

The Sun has now followed the Moon into your health and duties sector. Your leadership qualities will be noticed. Check that all mundane chores have been done today. Get a health check-up or review your eating and fitness habits. To take care of others you must first take care of yourself.

Thursday 23rd

Your partner sector is highlighted today. Spending time with a special person will bring satisfaction and maybe some surprises. You discover something about a lover or friend that takes you by surprise. This pleases you and brings you closer together. What can you build with this person?

Friday 24th

The Moon sits opposite Neptune so you must be careful that you are not creating a fog of illusion around you now. You are optimistic about a new connection but do not put them on a pedestal. Take off the rose-tinted glasses and see them for who they are.

Saturday 25th

Balancing two different aspects of life is not an easy task for you Pisces. You prefer to go with the flow and swim one way and then the other. However, today you may find that you are attempting to balance opposing points of view. Listen to both before deciding, Pisces.

Sunday 26th

Today you will have deep philosophical conversations. There may be an intellectual argument about the meaning of life, death and everything in between. You find this hard to discuss as you are not fixed on one train of thought. This is probably the best way to be about these subjects.

Monday 27th

There is a battle of the sexes going on today Pisces. Venus in your family sector is getting duped by Neptune. Do not let anyone fool you today. Also, Mars in your money sector is squaring off with Mercury who deals with commerce. A tense day, do not commit to anything.

Tuesday 28th

Dreams and illusions may get blown out of proportion today Pisces. The truth may be hidden from you. Do not let fools turn you upside down today. Maintain a perspective on something and keep it in your focus. Otherwise, your world may feel inverted. Liars and bullies are around you.

Wednesday 29th

Get career focused today Pisces. It is always good for you to plan ahead and create a career path. You get bored easily from working in one place and when the work stops fulfilling you, it is time to move on. You can aim higher than your colleagues Pisces.

Thursday 30th

Be careful not to get into heavy discussions today Pisces. You will find that you are out of your depth and will have to swim back to the shore for safety. Once something has come out of your mouth be sure to validate it or better still, say nothing at all.

Friday 31st

Today, you should let off some steam with your closest friends. Choose people who have known you most of your life and have proven that they are there for you when needed. You need a lift in spirits and a boost of confidence. These friends will be supportive.

AUGUST
. . . .

Saturday 1st
Mothers and fathers or roles of this kind will be in conflict today. Your nurturing side struggles with power issues coming from your social sector. It is impossible to balance this right now. You can talk the talk but you must put your money where your mouth is and show responsibility.

Sunday 2nd
The Sun in your duties sector needs you to be authentic in matters concerning communication. Your leadership qualities will be questioned if you wax and wane with an opinion. If you have promised to do something then do it or you could risk a tantrum from someone who relies on you.

Monday 3rd
Today there is a Full Moon in your sector of dreams and solitude. You may feel like running away and hiding from everyone. Naturally, you are drawn to be involved and on the front line but today this Moon seems to illuminate an overwhelming need to be alone.

Tuesday 4th

Issues that occur today can get out of hand. Mars is
in your money and value sector and squaring off with
Jupiter in your social sector. People will try to drain
all of your energy and drive but you will march on
relentlessly. Resist the urge to over-spend or over-eat.

Wednesday 5th

The Moon enters your sign and Mercury enters your
duties and service sectors. This is a great combination
for you as people will now take you seriously when you
say no. You will do only what is necessary as you suspect
that you may be on the brink of burnout.

Thursday 6th

Venus is just about finishing up in your family sector.
As she does so, she touches the point of fate and you
may make a wish for the future harmony of your closest
family. You know that the secret of a happy family is to
keep the communication loving.

Friday 7th

Today you feel more fired up and maybe a little selfish.
You may be planning a busy weekend where dining out
or trips to new places is involved. Venus enters your
creative sector and will become a nurturing influence on
your love affairs and art projects.

Saturday 8th

What an active Saturday you will have. There will be many chores to do alongside some experiences just for you. Today you find the balance needed to spend time being of service to others whilst doing things simply for the love of it. Well done, enjoy your day.

Sunday 9th

There is a little niggle today because the Moon is making an uneasy connection to those planets in your social sector. It makes you feel that you have neglected friendships and you may feel a little guilty. Ignore it, this is a test and it will soon pass.

Monday 10th

The Moon shifts and you may feel a little earthquake beneath your feet. There may have been something important you forgot to do over the weekend. Make time to do this today or it will eat away at you. This could be as simple as connecting by a phone call with someone.

Tuesday 11th

The struggle to balance your own needs with those of others returns today. You must learn to put yourself first Pisces. What you say does not gel with how you feel now. How can other people know what you want if you do not express it? Say it, Pisces.

Wednesday 12th

Make time today to chat with family, particularly your siblings. It seems that you all want to have a good rant and use each other as sounding boards. Family is your safe space to do this but be sure that they too are not taking advantage of your good nature.

Thursday 13th

Watch your temper today Pisces. It is not like you to blow like a volcano so if you do, this will be spectacular. You may be made to feel worthless by someone from your social sector. This could be an online argument in a group. Step away from the keyboard Pisces.

Friday 14th

There is pressure building inside you. Pacing the room muttering under your breath is not going to help. Go for a run, do something physical and get it out of your system. Alternatively, you may do something else grounded such as yoga or meditation. Get rid of that energy somehow.

Saturday 15th

Venus and the Moon meet up in your creative sector. You are much calmer and are soothed by this influence. There is lovely energy in the air from several planetary connections. This is perfect for love relationships. Romance is highlighted now and will make you feel great inside and out.

Sunday 16th

Try to hold on to that feeling from yesterday because today, Uranus the disruptor goes retrograde. You will find that you will be rushing about a bit more than usual. Uneasy energy from the Moon adds to the day but this will be over soon. Stay in that loved-up feeling.

Monday 17th

You can relax now. Today you must check in with your health and see what is lacking. You may need a boost of vitamins or immune support as recent tensions have drained your natural resources. You need to laugh today, find something to smile about and shine.

Tuesday 18th

Today there is a New Moon in your health and duties sector. A fitness class started now has a good chance of becoming part of your routine. You will enjoy this new challenge as it will be highly beneficial to you. Make this quality time for yourself Pisces.

Wednesday 19th

The Moon shifts into your relationship sector and you are drawn to spending time with people who mean a lot to you. This can also mean that your shadow side comes to the surface and you project your unwanted internal baggage onto others. You may need to face some demons.

Thursday 20th

Mercury enters your relationship sector. If there is someone special in your life, communication between the two of you will deepen. You will share dreams and visions together. Make sure that you stay real and do not let love blind you. Keep your feet on the ground please Pisces.

Friday 21st

What finances do you share with another person Pisces? This is a good day to evaluate your money obligations such as taxes or legacies. You must balance what is truly yours alone with what you are committed to with another. Harmony in your significant relationships is important to you.

Saturday 22nd

The Sun enters the sector of your chart that deals with other people and how you relate. This will add warmth and joy and will make your mission regarding boundaries somewhat easier. The Sun here can also herald a time where parts of you that you feel are unworthy can surface and be given credit.

Sunday 23rd

Travel and higher education come to your mind now and you are interested in courses of study that are a bit unusual. You tend to enjoy travelling by learning rather than visiting places. Religion, philosophy and foreign cultures can capture your imagination. Experience this from your own home Pisces.

Monday 24th

Unrest is the theme for today Pisces. You have plans and goals but feel restricted and unable to implement anything, however small. Communications may be misheard or misunderstood and you will find that you are repeating yourself in order to get your point across to someone who is not listening.

Tuesday 25th

Mercury lends you the gift of the gab and now your message is clear. However, another issue surfaces and there may be trouble with bosses or parental figures. This will also be a conflict between a lover and a friend. You must prioritise now Pisces. Spend time with those who nurture you.

Wednesday 26th

Venus and Jupiter are the two planets which bring luck and love and they are at odds today. This will continue the tension between your social sector and your creative sector. Put your energy into your creative pursuits and make yourself content with that. Let the naysayers walk on by.

Thursday 27th

This is a good day for love relationships. Venus is connecting with your co-ruler Neptune and together they make beautiful music. The atmosphere with a loved one can border on the surreal. It is not a bad thing to enjoy some fantasy time Pisces, so go with the flow today.

Friday 28th

The Moon is in your social sector and is making a helpful connection to Uranus. This can bring a pleasant surprise but remember, Uranus is in retrograde in your communications sector. You may have to make a lot of short trips or messages to get the surprise waiting for you.

Saturday 29th

This is a day with a lot of unsettled energy. It is not all bad though. You feel the restricting effects in your social sector but the power of speech given to you by Mercury means that you win the day. A friendship may be dissolved today. Barriers are breached.

Sunday 30th

You may feel tired today and would prefer to be left alone in the comfort of your own home. However, there will be someone who will try to demand your attention. This is a good chance for you to stick to your mission and say a gentle no, thank you.

Monday 31st

Personal achievements bring satisfaction today. You may reward yourself with a nice meal or a treat for your home. You feel like you are getting somewhere with your mission and are pleased with yourself. Take some time to congratulate yourself. Saying no does not have to be a negative thing.

SEPTEMBER

. . . .

Tuesday 1st

The Moon is in your sign again and emotional needs
turn to yourself. Mercury in your relationship sector is
talking to Pluto who likes transformation. Even though
Pluto is retrograde, he is pleased with your progress
so far this year. Old and outworn habits are being
transformed for the better.

Wednesday 2nd

A beautiful Full Moon lights up your own sign Pisces.
It is time for you to think about how you are doing with
your mission. What benefits have you gained? What still
needs a bit of work? Flirty Venus is being told to rein it
in by Saturn.

Thursday 3rd

Mercury now talks to Saturn. Love relationships are now
in focus for the boundaries lesson. Perhaps it is you that is
pushing too far now Pisces. Remember that other people
have boundaries too. It is your desire to merge deeply with
a loved one but be respectful and give them time.

Friday 4th

There is a battle of wills now as Venus and Mars are going head to head. Mars gets what Venus wants but right now he is on his own mission in the sign he rules. You must accept that there is time for yourself but time for a lover too. Today is one of those days where the lover comes first.

Saturday 5th

Mercury now flies into the sector of your chart which deals with sex, death, rebirth and shared finances. This will not be a comfortable time as a lot of hidden material may surface. Mercury is only attempting to heal this by making you aware of it. Nevertheless, it may be painful.

Sunday 6th

Venus also shifts signs now. She enters your health and duties sector where she will give you the strength to shine in your own right. You will take joy in carrying out mundane duties. The danger here is that you may become too fixated on goals and burn out.

Monday 7th

People want your attention today. There will be too much communication for you to deal with and too much for you to hold. You will either drop something heavy or throw it all up and say "enough!" Whatever the mood is today, it is guaranteed to be bigger than necessary.

Tuesday 8th

You desire to be with family today. Idle chit-chat or family gossip is what you need to take you away from your mission for a while. With family, you can dream and float around with a life-jacket on and know that you are safe. Come back to your mission after you have rested.

Wednesday 9th

Moon and Venus are talking together. You are a leading light when it comes to getting jobs done as this is no effort to you. Family may ask for favours and you happily agree. These are the times when you feel your worth. Unconditional love supports your day.

Thursday 10th

Mars goes retrograde today and you will feel a little sluggish for two months. He is in your sector of food, money and value. There could be digestive or money problems now. This will feel like a blockage so use this time to assess these areas of your life.

Friday 11th

The Sun opposes Neptune in your sign Pisces. This influence means that the fog or mist will be burned away from an illusion you have been harbouring. Neptune dissolves boundaries and allows you to merge with others but can lull you into a false sense of security. What is being made clear?

Saturday 12th

Today you will be facing your mission directly. Your heart has trouble reconciling the culling of friendships and you would rather not do it. This is for the best Pisces. You will realise just how much extra baggage you carry because you want to love and befriend every living soul.

Sunday 13th

You are feeling the first effects of the Mars retrograde today. There may be stomach problems or, in a figurative sense, you get a gut feeling about something. The good news for today is that Jolly Jupiter is now direct again and will help you in your social circle.

Monday 14th

You get extra sensitive due to a meeting between the Moon and Venus in your health and duties sector. Intuition combines with courage and you may act as a vessel for others to connect with their inner selves. You may also become a cheerleader and help someone get motivated.

Tuesday 15th

The Moon is once more in your relationship sector and you reminisce about past loves. This is a helpful process and you are able to resolve current problems with skills from the past. There will be some unrest in communications but you are able to soften the blow using compassionate words.

Wednesday 16th

You may become hot-headed today and try to force your
will on another. This is not like you so you must look
at the trigger and ask yourself how this has happened.
Conditioning from your past may have to be un-learned
now as it no longer serves your best interests.

Thursday 17th

A New Moon in your relationship sector gives you the
chance to make affirmations regarding how you relate
to others. This is part and parcel of your 2020 mission
to make use of all that you have learned so far. This will
help you grow.

Friday 18th

Today you may feel that something is one-sided and
tipping the balance you are trying to achieve. You wonder
if you have gone too far with your mission? Be assured
that you have not, the imbalance you are feeling is the
load you have made lighter and you are unused to it.

Saturday 19th

The Moon connects to Saturn and Pluto in your social
sector. Guilt will creep in and try to make you feel bad
about letting people down. You must turn that around
Pisces. You have lifted yourself up. Be careful that this
guilty feeling does not manifest in a health problem.

Sunday 20th

The Moon drifts into your travel sector and opposes disruptive Uranus. You will find it hard to talk to people today. Get yourself a good fantasy book, watch a film or documentary and let yourself travel in your mind. Be stubborn, shut the door and stay home.

Monday 21st

Let work or career take your mind off things today. You have not thought about your career goals for a while so use today to make an action plan and see what you come up with. This is not the time to talk to your boss so keep it private for now.

Tuesday 22nd

The Sun now enters your sector of sex, death and rebirth. This is a welcome influence as you prefer to have some light when exploring the darker mysteries of life. Mercury is here and has tried to probe his way through, now the Sun lights his way out.

Wednesday 23rd

Once more you are being reminded about boundaries. Mercury is connecting to Saturn who tells him enough is enough. No more exploration here. Mercury also rules commerce so you may want to check any finances you have with another person. Are you still committed to this investment?

Thursday 24th

You struggle with getting on with things today. Mars in his retrograde is opposite flighty Mercury. The Warrior is feeling stuck in your money and value house. What is yours and what is another person's? At the moment, shared finances are available to you whilst personal ones are not. Think carefully before you spend Pisces.

Friday 25th

Your social sector gets a big hit today. Jupiter brings fun and laughter but Pluto and Saturn come in and suck it all away. There is a dark shadow hanging over your friendships now but look carefully, this is coming from you. Your unnecessary guilt is preventing you from being light and free.

Saturday 26th

Luckily, the Moon shifts just in time and you now feel like you are seeing your tribe for the first time. The time-wasters and energy vampires are dropping away. You are beginning to see where your empathic qualities have been a source of exhaustion.

Sunday 27th

Mercury dives into your travel sector where he will have a grand time opening your eyes to new things. You may not actually travel but you will pick up an interest in foreign cultures now. Gathering and sharing information with your social circle becomes a pleasurable activity.

Monday 28th

The Moon is once again in your sign. Emotions can be turned inwards or simply not revealed. Alone time is enjoyable and you take comfort in indulgences such as a favourite TV show or book. Take this time to re-connect with yourself and spirit. Prayer and meditation will create a good environment for self-nurturing.

Tuesday 29th

Saturn now turns direct. The planet of Karma hopes that you have listened well to the lessons this year. If you have not, then that hard lesson on boundaries will come back in another form. Venus gives Mars a helping hand and you feel some forward motion today with your finances.

Wednesday 30th

Now that Saturn is direct, the first thing he does is to connect with Mars. He tells him that he has spent too much and eaten too much. This is why he cannot move as fast as he likes. Aggression is felt but cannot be expressed today. Let it go Pisces.

OCTOBER

. . . .

Thursday 1st

October begins with a Full Moon in your money sector.
This will highlight a few things from the last six months.
The most important thing here is that your sense of self-
worth is showing itself now. You have worked hard on
boundary issues and not being walked over.

Friday 2nd

Venus the planet of love and harmony enters your
relationship sector. This is great news for you. Venus
will see that your love relationships are balanced and
harmonised while she is here. Pay attention to all the
subtle love nuances now. Happy days!

Saturday 3rd

A delicious connection from the Moon to Venus
means that romance is most definitely in the air today.
Good food, wine and company are on the menu for
a sensual evening. If you are single then indulge
yourself with all your favourites.

Sunday 4th

You have a pause from your romantic place today. The Moon sits opposite Mercury who wants to delve deep into another person's secrets. You may be holding back a bit now and this will cause a wobble in your vulnerable love-life. Choose how far to go, remember boundaries.

Monday 5th

Good news, Pluto is now direct. If you have learned the lesson of not giving your power away to everyone, then this shift will be welcome in your love life. Someone is inviting you to be more intimate, can you do this without falling back on old habits Pisces?

Tuesday 6th

The telephones buzz today as your family are ever active and chatty. Maybe someone has news and all the family are sharing this at the same time. You enjoy the random, light-hearted conversations with siblings. You will even enjoy the teasing and mock fighting. You have a very communicative family.

Wednesday 7th

Mercury sits opposite Uranus today and this influence means that you have to watch what you say. This can be Mercury motormouth speaking out of turn. It can also mean that he has probed too far and is being given a warning to back off. Please respect this Pisces.

Thursday 8th

The Moon slips into a more nurturing sign which for you is covered by your creative sector. Today, try to do things which are soul food for you. Creative expression in the form of art or poetry would be good. Better still, dedicate this to a muse and thrill your lover.

Friday 9th

You may find that control issues surface today but you know how to deal with this now don't you? Saying no from a place of compassion leads to the greatest respect for both parties. The Moon and Venus help you to do this. Well done Pisces, what a transformation.

Saturday 10th

Your lover may surprise you today with another evening out. Venus connects to Uranus in a helpful way which means that surprises and not shocks will occur. You may be making many trips and messages in the day but the evening will be sensual and relaxing. Nurture your taste buds now.

Sunday 11th

Be careful today. You or someone close to you can be rather unstable emotionally. Be kind and thoughtful as this is just a passing moon phase and will not last. It has no basis in reality and is therefore not a serious issue. Do not dig for answers today.

Monday 12th

Mercury is soon to go on another retrograde mission so today, remember to back up your devices and double-check travel plans. Now is not the time to sign new contracts or make commitments. Bide your time as this retrograde will cover sectors dealing with deep issues and shared finances.

Tuesday 13th

The Moon enters your relationship sector now. Try not to make too many plans with a loved one as they are likely to be disrupted now. Keep it low-key, close to home and on a level that will not cause any unrest. Take it slowly and keep the fire on a low burn.

Wednesday 14th

Mercury retrograde begins. The Moon and Venus sit together to watch the show from your relationship sector. A simple romantic comedy is just the thing for a mid-week rendezvous. Nothing fancy or expensive. Simply a homely, uncomplicated evening with food and a movie. Make everyone's favourite comfort foods.

Thursday 15th

What have you learned concerning power struggles this year? This may be the first test from Pluto and in a Mercury retrograde too! Pluto needs to see something demolished and rebuilt. This is a time of endings and beginnings. Consider what has outlived its usefulness in your life now.

Friday 16th

Today's New Moon gives you a hint at what needs to be transformed. What is out of balance now? What deep issues do you choose to ignore because you are too scared to deal with them? Balance needs to be restored by your own hands or Pluto will do it for you.

Saturday 17th

The Moon makes connections to Mercury and Uranus and this influence will make you say what is on your mind. Mercury is retrograde and in the deep, intense sign of Scorpio. You may push or be pushed too far today. If it is too uncomfortable, don't go there.

Sunday 18th

You will be satisfied with your progress on your mission. Today you can sit back and assess how far you have come. You have changed many things for the better and lightened your load Pisces. What an achievement. You can still be the empathic, caring friend but now you know your limits.

Monday 19th

Venus and Mars are fighting for a bit of Jupiter's good fortune. For you, this means that men and women may be in a friendly challenge today. Women, with Venus' aid, will win this one. This battle involves your money sector and your 'other' sector. Which side are you on?

Tuesday 20th

More tense energy today as Mercury retrograde sits opposite Uranus in your money and value sector. There may be rows about what you own and what is shared with another. This is another of the retrograde influences. Keep calm and resist the need to prove yourself right.

Wednesday 21st

Venus is sweet-talking Pluto today. She is persuading him that something in your relationship sector needs to change. She wants it done her way and is asking Pluto to help. Watch out for sneaky control issues in your relationship. If it is not that serious, let it happen, you may like it.

Thursday 22nd

The Sun now begins its month stay in your travel sector. Here, you will discover a fascination for other cultures, higher education and possibly taboo subjects like sex, death and rebirth. The occult attracts you now. Expand your mind, it will be good for you.

Friday 23rd

You are emotionally driven to be with friendship groups which stand for a good cause today. You get out your soapbox and make a speech loaded with emotion. Your words will fall on deaf ears. Do you really want to raise a revolution Pisces? Step down and concentrate on your lover now instead.

Saturday 24th

Venus now turns her attention to Saturn. Someone around you, most likely your lover, will push a little further through your comfort zone. This is ok because you are learning to accept your limits and will know it when they are triggered. This is a good test of your convictions.

Sunday 25th

Mercury has nothing to say today as he is in the heart of the Sun and listening. The Moon enters your sign and you feel more moody than usual. This is time for you to drift off into your own world and listen like Mercury is. Connect to spirit now.

Monday 26th

The Moon in your sign is making helpful connections to the Sun, Mercury and Uranus. You will hear something to your advantage. This will come from deep inside you or another person. You may even hear the voice of 'God' now. Keep this information to yourself until the retrograde is over.

Tuesday 27th

The Moon now sits on top of Neptune and further deepens the surreal, spiritual atmosphere going on within you. Do not be fooled by false prophets. You may drift too far today so do something grounding and stay connected to this planet. Physical exercise or yoga will help.

Wednesday 28th

Today you have Venus and Mercury both entering your sex, death and rebirth sector from either end. Mercury is of course still retrograde. They appear to call out to each other. Venus wants to know the secrets that Mercury has unearthed. It is crucial that you are discreet today Pisces.

Thursday 29th

The Moon pays a visit to sulky Mars in your money sector. You may have a setback with finances that cause you to regret some spending from earlier in the year. There is nothing you can do about it. Get through the day by doing something Mars likes. Exercise helps.

Friday 30th

You are contemplating your future based on your past. Conversations with siblings can bring up a lot of memories. You wonder if your current situation is a result of your past efforts and focus on the mistakes. Turn that around and celebrate your successes Pisces. Do not dumb yourself down.

Saturday 31st

A Full Moon in your communications sector brings things to a conclusion. The Sun opposes Uranus and you get an 'aha' moment. The Moon sits on top of Uranus and you feel it deeply. A moment of regret comes over you as you feel a chapter has exposed itself and is now closing.

NOVEMBER
·················

Sunday 1st
There may still be some spooky surprises for you today Pisces. The Halloween Full Moon has left the Sun shining right in the face of Uranus. You will get a 'Eureka!' moment where something now becomes blindingly obvious. There will be happy communication today too. You will hear some good news.

Monday 2nd
Your family sector gets triggered today. The Moon connects to Saturn and it is likely that you will hear some good advice from an elder in the family. Saturn reminds you of your boundaries and is pleased that you are putting them in place. Teachers may also feature.

Tuesday 3rd
A lovely connection between the Moon, Mars and Venus means that interactions between men and women go well today. Family can be fun and full of laughter and the mood is much lighter than it has been. Several generations may gather together. Enjoy each other's company Pisces.

Wednesday 4th

Mercury, at last, goes direct again. He will journey back over parts of your sex, death and rebirth sector then continue his mission in your travel and higher education sector. Maybe you have taken this time to review these areas. Both of these areas are deep and uncomfortable for you Pisces.

Thursday 5th

Your love life and artistic pursuits are in the spotlight now. These could be the same thing. You may be in love with art, music or literature. There will be a little difficulty getting things to the standard you desire today. Don't lose heart, put it aside for another time.

Friday 6th

Today you feel tired and have no energy. Your creative urges are just not going the way you want and it is making you weary. This is better than making your frustrated and angry which it could well do. Use this time to rest up and look again with fresh eyes.

Saturday 7th

Health should be your main topic today Pisces. If you have been cooped up indoors too much lately, take a brisk walk outdoors. Fresh air will fill your lungs and make you feel good. You may lead an expedition to a new place. Be child-like today, surprise yourself.

Sunday 8th

Today's energy is of a fixed nature which will feel uncomfortable to you who likes to go with the flow. It will feel rigid and restrictive. Someone may have made plans that cannot be changed. There is a danger of you having a tantrum now Pisces. Do what you are told today.

Monday 9th

The Moon enters your opposite sign and your important relationships become your focus. This may not be a good thing because the celestial lovers are sitting opposite each other and remember, Mars is in retrograde. Women may be persuasive or bossy but either way they have the upper hand today.

Tuesday 10th

Mercury hits the very last degree of your sex, death and rebirth sector. This area also deals with shared finances. Anything you committed to over the last few weeks is now up for a final review. This is a take-it-or-leave-it time. It is probably best to leave it.

Wednesday 11th

You have taken Mercury's advice and are now assessing money that you have tied up with another person. You will be aiming to balance out what is yours and what belongs to someone else. You find that you are implementing the lessons from the planets in your social sector.

Thursday 12th
The Moon sits with Venus today and together they help you to reconcile all that may have gone awry during the Mercury retrograde. You are sensitive and loving. Deep feelings come up but they do not bother you. Awareness is the first step to dealing with them.

Friday 13th
Today Jupiter and Pluto meet in your social sector. This means that big changes can be made without trauma. These changes are likely connected to friendships. You handle this exceptionally well. Something old and outworn has become a new thing of beauty. This is a treasure for you Pisces.

Saturday 14th
Mars gets his boots back on and turns direct. At last, you see forward motion and become more assertive in the area of money, self-worth and beauty. He is in his own sign and will do his very best for you while he is here. Energy levels will pick up and new projects started. All systems are go now.

Sunday 15th
Today's New Moon is an excellent time to use that Mars energy to make new plans, intentions and goals. The Moon is in the other sign Mars rules, Scorpio. Anything begun now has a high chance of success. Intensity and power are yours to use if you so choose now.

Monday 16th

Venus is squaring off to the planets in your social sector but this time she is not going to get her way. You may find that someone comes creeping back to attempt to renew a friendship with you. You must be strong and stick to your convictions.

Tuesday 17th

You are at a standstill today and looking back at the past, maybe the recent past. There is a chance of getting into an argument today. Mercury is opposite Uranus which means that everyone needs to watch what they say and think before they speak.

Wednesday 18th

The Moon in your social sector makes an uneasy connection to Mars. Perhaps he is marching onwards and leaving something behind. This will make you feel like you have left good friends behind. March on Pisces, you are doing the right thing.

Thursday 19th

The Sun in your travel sector is talking to Saturn. Think about boundaries when Saturn is involved. This time, stretching your boundaries and exploring other lands is the theme. Saturn encourages you to grow within reasonable limits if it means that you are educated. Where will you go?

Friday 20th

Time to dream now. You have been given a passport by Saturn and you can now explore your fantasies. You are surprised by your urge to go beyond your comfort zones. People may try to dissuade you. This is the time for you to grow in another direction Pisces.

Saturday 21st

The Sun now warms up your career sector. This could herald a time where career and travel are combined. You may be asked to go on a business trip. Venus gets sexy in your travel sector today too. Does the exotic and erotic attract you? Is this your new mission?

Sunday 22nd

The Moon enters your sign and your heart beats a little faster with new ideas. There is something in the air which excites you now. This could be new journeys, courses or a change of career. Whatever it is, it is putting a much-needed spring in your step.

Monday 23rd

The Moon makes lovely connections today which lighten your spirit. She sits with Neptune who likes to dissolve boundaries. At this time, he is taking down your personal reservations about stepping out further in life. The Moon is also talking to your social sector, do you have friends abroad?

Tuesday 24th

Mercury rather likes this new-found courage of yours and gets all the information from Neptune. He begins to scan the depths of your travel sector and believes that the more unusual cultures will suit you best. The Moon in your money sector looks at the financial side for you.

Wednesday 25th

You may start a savings plan for your new travel ideas. Put some money aside and build on it until the time is right. Listen to your dreams now as they will give you a hint as to where you would benefit the most. Dream symbols are the clues.

Thursday 26th

You are raring to go. The new plans you have been forming in your mind are exciting you. You may feel like a runner at the start of a race, filled with anticipation and adrenaline. Hold back Pisces, you are just at the planning stages of this bold new adventure.

Friday 27th

The tension continues as the Moon sits with Uranus and they both sit opposite Venus. She is bewitching you with tales from exotic lands. You may be frustrated that you cannot do anything about this right now. Uranus gets you jumpy today. Calm down Pisces.

Saturday 28th

You have further confirmation that this new, exciting adventure is right for you. Neptune, your co-ruler wants his little fish to swim far and wide. The ocean is far too big to stay only in one place. You have permission to explore the warmer or colder seas.

Sunday 29th

The planets in your social sector now give you their blessings too. The lesson this year regarding boundaries taught you that personal ones must be protected. Now it is teaching you that your world and its physical boundaries are there to be explored. The excitement is building.

Monday 30th

Today there is a Full Moon in your family sector. Something will come to a head and be completed now. You inform your family of any new plans and receive their encouragement. One warning though, not everyone will be happy for you. A lunar eclipse throws a shadow over you.

DECEMBER

. . . .

Tuesday 1st

You get extra help with planning any career moves now, especially if they concern travel. Mercury enters your career sector and will assist you in researching these areas. This will be a fantastic opportunity to put your ideas out there to the boss. Put the feelers out now Pisces.

Wednesday 2nd

Nurture yourself today with some home comforts. You may also want to spend time on your artistic projects as these also give you food for your soul. Today is also favourable for snuggling down with a loved one and enjoying each other's company in the safety of your home.

Thursday 3rd

Today you find that emotions and actions are not in sync. You try to find the enthusiasm to get on with things but do not have the energy or inclination. As long as the more important tasks are done, leave the smaller ones for another time.

Friday 4th

Your energy levels have picked up and you will be going about your duty with a cheery smile. Nothing can keep you down for long. The Moon and Mercury are exchanging messages and both are on task to make your travel and career plans a real possibility.

Saturday 5th

The Moon in your health and duties sector gives Mars the energetic kick he needs. Money talks are possible today. Could this be a promotion Pisces? Be careful when communicating as someone may want to rock your boat today. There is stubbornness in the air, are you the immovable one?

Sunday 6th

Venus is gracing your travel sector with her beauty and harmony. She also rules money. Today she talks to the planet of dreams, Neptune. Together they help you to consider the money options for your next mission. You also think about the pros and cons of such an adventure.

Monday 7th

Today you may need to discuss things with a lover or important person in your life. You will be going over the finer details of your plans. This is a step-up for you as this is something you don't like doing. This person may surprise you with their experience.

Tuesday 8th

A connection from the Moon to the planets in your social sector encourages you to be with like-minded people today. Saturn sits at the final critical degree of this sector for the next ten days. It is crucial that you use this time to review the lessons you have learned on boundaries.

Wednesday 9th

Do not get fooled today Pisces. You may become so fixated on something that you fail to see the shortcomings. Bad advice or discouragement may come your way. Step to one side and view this with eyes wide open. Something that is too good to be true usually isn't true.

Thursday 10th

Sexy Venus in your travel sector flirts with Pluto, the planet of change. If you have friends abroad or with great influence, you may connect with these now. There could be an open invitation to visit. Do your homework first, weigh it all up and if it looks good, go for it.

Friday 11th

The Moon now also enters your travel sector. Be mindful that you can become overly attached to a plan that stirs your emotions. Your interest in the exotic and erotic grows and you may surprise yourself by finding a new passion in the deeper mysteries of life.

Saturday 12th

The Moon and Venus share the same spot in the sky and this too is in your travel sector. You may have never before considered foreign culture as something that would attract you but here it is, filling your heart with longing. Mars gives you the energy to focus on the money needed.

Sunday 13th

This new mission to explore is gifted to you by the planetary positions in your chart Pisces. The Moon is in a sign which deals with higher education and foreign travel but also in your career sector. Remember Saturn sitting at that last degree? It is time to approach the boss Pisces.

Monday 14th

Here is the golden opportunity that you have been
waiting for. A New Moon in the sign of travel and the
area of career urges you to set this plan in motion.
Venus and Jupiter, who are known for their blessing, are
connecting and sending you lots of luck.

Tuesday 15th

Beautiful Venus steps into your career sector. What more
can you ask for Pisces? There will be peace and harmony
in the workplace. As she also rules money, this heralds
a good time for you to make a solid action plan. Your
words and energy are in sync today.

Wednesday 16th

For the next two and a half years, Saturn will be
travelling through your sector of dreams and isolation.
There will be tough lessons to learn now. You will learn
how to be alone but not lonely. Your inner rebel may
surface and there will be good causes that interest you.

Thursday 17th

The Moon makes great connections with Jupiter and
Saturn today. You will feel gratitude for their influence
on you this year. Think of these as the best teachers and
guides you can have. Take the time today to acknowledge
the gifts they have given you to help you grow.

Friday 18th

Mercury is quiet today as he sits in the heart of the
Sun. Now is your chance to listen Pisces. Take in all the
information you need for future career plans. Research,
collate and sort through any data you have gathered
which may be of use to you.

Saturday 19th

The Moon enters your sign and you will feel reflective. Jolly
Jupiter is at the last degree of your social sector. Today there
will be fun with special friends but with Jupiter here, he is
just giving you a warning that he expands what he touches.
Don't overdo the food and drink!

Sunday 20th

Jupiter says goodbye to your social sector and bounces into your dreams. He will stay here for a year and you will enjoy his many blessings. He greets Saturn as he does so. Fathers and sons may feature and you will see reconciliation or renewed commitment to elders or authority figures.

Monday 21st

The Winter Solstice occurs today. The longest, darkest night is the best time to reflect on the past year. You will feel sociable and need to get out with friends. Self-sacrifice is your default and you may return to it, but only for a moment.

Tuesday 22nd

The Solstice brought the Sun to your social sector. This is great timing as you will get a good idea of how your friendship circles have now changed for the better. You will become a leader of sorts and great respect comes your way. Well done Pisces, be proud of yourself now.

Wednesday 23rd

You may feel a little edgy today. The Moon sits with Mars and you may be spending too much. They both connect to Pluto who tells you to take control of this spending. It is Christmas and this is quite normal but your planetary allies cannot help but warn you.

Thursday 24th

Now the eating, drinking and parties are starting. The Moon is in your communications sector and is typically adding to the mood of the season. In this sector, you make many short trips and messages. The Moon here likes the good things in life and you deserve them.

Friday 25th

Happy Christmas Pisces. There are so many surprises coming your way. Fathers, sons, friends and lovers will gather today and make your day special. The Moon sits with Uranus indicating surprise but be careful as this may also be tension and irritability. This is all typical of the season.

Saturday 26th

Today you may be recovering from the night before. The Moon connects to Neptune your co-ruler. Neptune can influence time spent alone in another world. There is also a chance that you are asked to be your old self and self-sacrifice. The Moon also connects to Pluto who gives you the power to say no.

Sunday 27th

Family time is still on the agenda. Perhaps you have a large family and the season dictates a lot of visits to relatives. Siblings can provide fun and laughter today. Go with the flow and let your inner child come out to play.

Monday 28th

You will be thinking about, and sharing your visions and dreams with family now. You may have some resistance from people who think it is a bad move. Listen to what they are saying and respect their opinion as you are having some guilt about this. Let this mood pass.

Tuesday 29th

Just before the year ends, there is a Full Moon in your creative sector. Mother figures are in the spotlight now. An artistic project with which you nurture yourself may have come to completion now and you can celebrate it. Love affairs are also illuminated under this Moon.

Wednesday 30th

How do you nurture and how do you provide Pisces? There may be questions today regarding how your new vision of travelling will benefit you financially. You may be thinking if it is even viable. You get a moment of conflicting emotions. Hold them but know that these will pass soon.

Thursday 31st

The end of the year arrives and you take a good look back at 2020. You will feel emotional about the necessary losses of the year. You may not have the energy to party the year away Pisces. Be good to yourself and recall how much you have grown. Enjoy 2021.

Pisces

. . . .

PEOPLE WHO
SHARE YOUR SIGN

PEOPLE WHO
SHARE YOUR SIGN

No pinch can take the faraway sign of Pisces out of their dreamland. With their artistic flair, compassionate hearts, and wonderful imaginations, Pisceans can both inspire and heal. Whether it's sharing their visionary talents like Alexander McQueen and Jenny Packham, or emotional lyrics like Kurt Cobain and Johnny Cash, the gifts from Pisceans can help restore a magic to the world. Discover which of these enchanting Pisceans share your exact birthday and see if you can spot the similarities.

February 20th

Rihanna (1988), Miles Teller (1987), Trevor Noah (1984), Chelsea Peretti (1978), Kurt Cobain (1967, Cindy Crawford (1966), Walter Becker (1950), Ivana Trump (1949), Mitch McConnell (1942)

February 21st

Sophie Turner (1996), Riyad Mahrez (1991), Ashley Greene (1987), Ellen Page (1987), Mélanie Laurent (1983), Jennifer Love Hewitt (1979), Jordan Peele (1979), Michael McIntyre (1976), Kelsey Grammar (1955), Alan Rickman (1946), Nina Simone (1933), Hubert de Givenchy (1927)

February 22nd

Drew Barrymore (1975), James Blunt (1974), Chris Moyles (1974), Jeri Ryan (1968), Steve Irwin (1962), Kyle MacLachlan (1959), Julie Walters (1950), Niki Lauda (1949), Robert Kardashian (1944), Bruce Forsyth (1928)

February 23rd

Dakota Fanning (1994), Skylar Grey (1986), Andre Ward (1984), Aziz Ansari (1983), Emily Blunt (1983), Josh Gad (1981), Kelly Macdonald (1976), Daymond John (1969), W. E. B. Du Bois (1868)

February 24th
Earl Sweatshirt (1994), O'Shea Jackson Jr. (1991), Priscilla Chan (1985), Floyd Mayweather (1977), Bonnie Somerville (1974), Billy Zane (1966), Kristin Davis (1965), Steve Jobs (1955), Phil Knight (1938)

February 25th
Eugenie Bouchard (1994), Rashida Jones (1976), Chelsea Handler (1975), Sean Astin (1971), Téa Leoni (1966), George Harrison (1943), Anthony Burgess (1917), Pierre-Auguste Renoir (1841)

February 26th
CL (1991), Charley Webb (1988), Teresa Palmer (1986), Erykah Badu (1971), Max Martin (1971), Recep Tayyip Erdoğan, President of Turkey (1954), Michael Bolton (1953), Johnny Cash (1932), Victor Hugo (1802)

February 27th
Lindsey Morgan (1990), JWoww (1986), Kate Mara (1983), Josh Groban (1981), Chelsea Clinton (1980), Peter Andre (1973), Li Bingbing (1973), Derren Brown (1971), Timothy Spall (1957), Elizabeth Taylor (1932), John Steinbeck (1902)

February 28th

Sarah Bolger (1991), Olivia Palermo (1986), Karolína
Kurková (1984), Natalia Vodianova (1982), Ali Larter (1976),
Amanda Abbington (1974), Ainsley Harriott (1957), Paul
Krugman (1953), Bernadette Peters (1948), Frank Gehry
(1929)

February 29th

Jessie T. Usher (1992), Mark Foster (1984), Ja Rule (1976),
Pedro Sánchez, Prime Minister of Spain (1972), Tony
Robbins (1960), Dennis Farina (1944)

March 1st

Justin Bieber (1994), Kesha (1987), Lupita Nyong'o (1983),
Shahid Afridi (1980), Jensen Ackles (1978), Javier Bardem
(1969), Paul Hollywood (1966), Zack Snyder (1966), Ron
Howard (1954), Harry Belafonte (1927), Harry Winston
(1896), Frédéric Chopin (1810)

March 2nd

Becky G (1997), Nathalie Emmanuel (1989), Bryce Dallas
Howard (1981), Rebel Wilson (1980), Chris Martin (1977),
Alexander Armstrong (1970), Daniel Craig (1968), Jon
Bon Jovi (1962), Karen Carpenter (1950), Lou Reed (1942),
Dr. Seuss (1904)

March 3rd

Camila Cabello (1997), Nathalie Kelley (1985), Jessica Biel (1982), Ronan Keating (1977), Alison King (1973), Julie Bowen (1970), Ira Glass (1959), Miranda Richardson (1958), Zico (1953), Alexander Graham Bell (1847)

March 4th

Brooklyn Beckham (1999), Bobbi Kristina Brown (1993), Draymond Green (1990), Whitney Port (1985), Chaz Bono (1969), Patsy Kensit (1968), Sam Taylor-Johnson (1967), Tim Vine (1967), Khaled Hosseini (1965), Patricia Heaton (1958), Catherine O'Hara (1954), Shakin' Stevens (1948)

March 5th

Madison Beer (1999), Taylor Hill (1996), Sterling Knight (1989), Dan Carter (1982), Hanna Alström (1981), Jolene Blalock (1975), Eva Mendes (1974), John Frusciante (1970), Lisa Robin Kelly (1970), Joel Osteen (1963), Talia Balsam (1959), Esther Hicks (1948)

March 6th

Tyler, The Creator (1991), Agnieszka Radwańska (1989), Shaquille O'Neal (1972), Connie Britton (1967), Rob Reiner (1947), David Gilmour (1946), Valentina Tereshkova (1937), Gabriel García Márquez (1927), Michelangelo (1475)

March 7th
Laura Prepon (1980), Jenna Fischer (1974), Matthew
Vaughn (1971), Rachel Weisz (1970), Wanda Sykes (1964),
E. L. James (1963), Bryan Cranston (1956), Piet Mondrian
(1872)

March 8th
Stephanie Davis (1993), Petra Kvitová (1990), Kat Von
D (1982), James Van Der Beek (1977), Freddie Prinze Jr.
(1976), Florentino Pérez, (1947), Randy Meisner (1946)

March 9th
Bow Wow (1987), Brittany Snow (1986), Matthew Gray
Gubler (1980), Oscar Isaac (1979), YG (1969), Juliette
Binoche (1964), Bobby Fischer (1943), Yuri Gagarin (1934)

March 10th
Emily Osment (1992), Ivan Rakitic (1988), Olivia Wilde
(1984), Carrie Underwood (1983), Samuel Eto'o (1981),
Robin Thicke (1977), Timbaland (1972), Jon Hamm (1971),
Sharon Stone (1958), Chuck Norris (1940)

March 11th

Thora Birch (1982), Letoya Luckett (1981), Benji Madden (1979), Joel Madden (1979), Didier Drogba (1978), Johnny Knoxville (1971), Terrence Howard (1969), John Barrowman (1967), Jenny Packham (1965), Alex Kingston (1963), Rupert Murdoch (1931)

March 12th

Christina Grimmie (1994), Stromae (1985), Jaimie Alexander (1984), Pete Doherty (1979), Aaron Eckhart (1968), James Taylor (1948), Liza Minnelli (1946), Jack Kerouac (1922)

March 13th

Jordyn Jones (2000), Mikaela Shiffrin (1995), Kaya Scodelario (1992), Tristan Thompson (1991), Common (1972), Jorge Sampaoli (1960), Dana Delany (1956), William H. Macy (1950)

March 14th

Simone Biles (1997), Ansel Elgort (1994), Stephen Curry (1988), Jamie Bell (1986), Taylor Hanson (1983), Chris Klein (1979), Brian Quinn (1976), Megan Follows (1968), Billy Crystal (1948), Michael Caine (1933), Quincy Jones (1933), Albert Einstein (1879)

March 15th
Paul Pogba (1993), Lil Dicky (1988), Jai Courtney (1986), Kellan Lutz (1985), Eva Longoria (1975), will.i.am (1975), Bret Michaels (1963), Fabio Lanzoni (1959), Mike Love (1941), Ruth Bader Ginsburg (1933), Gerda Wegener (1886)

March 16th
Wolfgang Van Halen (1991), Theo Walcott (1989), Jhené Aiko (1988), Alexandra Daddario (1986), Danny Brown (1981), Brooke Burns (1978), Sophie Hunter (1978), Alan Tudyk (1971), Lauren Graham (1967), Flavor Flav (1959), Victor Garber (1949), Jerry Lewis (1926)

March 17th
John Boyega (1992), Hozier (1990), Grimes (1988), Rob Kardashian (1987), Edin Džeko (1986), Coco Austin (1979), Brittany Daniel (1976), Alexander McQueen (1969), Billy Corgan (1967), Rob Lowe (1964), Gary Sinise (1955), Kurt Russell (1951), Pattie Boyd (1944), Nat King Cole (1919)

March 18th
Lily Collins (1989), Danneel Ackles (1979), Adam Levine (1979), Alex Jones (1977), Emma Willis (1976), Queen Latifah (1970), Peter Jones (1966), Vanessa Williams (1963), Grover Cleveland, 22nd and 24th US President (1837)

March 19th

Héctor Bellerín (1995), Garrett Clayton (1991), AJ Lee (1987), Bianca Balti (1984), Eduardo Saverin (1982), Kolo Touré (1981), Bruce Willis (1955), Glenn Close (1947), Ursula Andress (1936), David Livingstone (1813)

March 20th

Marcos Rojo (1990), Ruby Rose (1986), iJustine (1984), Fernando Torres (1984), Freema Agyeman (1979), Chester Bennington (1976), Michael Rapaport (1970), Kathy Ireland (1963), David Thewlis (1963), Holly Hunter (1958), Spike Lee (1957), Sting (1951), Douglas Tompkins (1943-2015), Fred Rogers (1928), B. F. Skinner (1904)